Faculty Collaboration:
Enhancing the Quality of Scholarship and Teaching

by Ann E. Austin and Roger G. Baldwin

ASHE-ERIC Higher Education Report No. 7, 1991

Prepared by

Clearinghouse on Higher Education
The George Washington University

In cooperation with

Association for the Study
of Higher Education

Published by

School of Education and Human Development
The George Washington University

Jonathan D. Fife, Series Editor

Cite as

Austin, Ann E., and Roger G. Baldwin. 1991. *Faculty Collaboration: Enhancing the Quality of Scholarship and Teaching.* ASHE-ERIC Higher Education Report No. 7. Washington, D.C.: The George Washington University, School of Education and Human Development.

Library of Congress Catalog Card Number 92-81699
ISSN 0884-0040
ISBN 1-878380-12-5

Managing Editor: Bryan Hollister
Manuscript Editor: Barbara Fishel, Editech
Cover design by Michael David Brown, Rockville, Maryland

The ERIC Clearinghouse on Higher Education invites individuals to submit proposals for writing monographs for the *ASHE-ERIC Higher Education Report* series. Proposals must include:
1. A detailed manuscript proposal of not more than five pages.
2. A chapter-by-chapter outline.
3. A 75-word summary to be used by several review committees for the initial screening and rating of each proposal.
4. A vita and a writing sample.

ERIC **Clearinghouse on Higher Education**
School of Education and Human Development
The George Washington University
One Dupont Circle, Suite 630
Washington, DC 20036-1183

This publication was prepared partially with funding from the Office of Educational Research and Improvement, U.S. Department of Education, under contract no. ED RI-88-062014. The opinions expressed in this report do not necessarily reflect the positions or policies of OERI or the Department.

EXECUTIVE SUMMARY

Faculty collaboration has grown dramatically over the course of this century. Conventional stereotypes, which convey the image of professors conducting research in the isolation of a laboratory or teaching alone in front of a room of passive students, overlook important aspects of modern academic life. Many professors now do much of their work—teaching, conducting research, and writing—in partnership with colleagues.

Faculty collaboration occurs in a variety of settings and takes different forms, depending on the nature of the collaborative team and the goals of its members. Essentially, faculty collaboration is a cooperative endeavor that involves common goals, coordinated effort, and outcomes or products for which the collaborators share responsibility and credit. This definition is broad and flexible, because faculty collaboration varies in numerous ways contingent upon whether the partnership is for teaching or research as well as on the participants' fields of specialization, institutions of employment, career stages, and a host of other factors.

Professors choose to work in concert with colleagues for numerous reasons. Many believe collaboration increases productivity, maintains motivation, and stimulates creativity and risk taking. It can maximize the use of limited resources and could enhance the quality of teaching and research. Sometimes complex problems accompany faculty collaboration, however, such as difficulty concerning evaluation and assigning credit for work produced in collaboration. Because of the increasing popularity of faculty collaboration and the complex questions it poses to higher education, the time is right for a comprehensive examination of this important topic.

Why Is Faculty Collaboration a Growing Trend?

The growth of collaboration is not limited to the academic sector. Indeed, higher education is in the midst of a larger movement that is sweeping across our society. For example, teaming is increasingly prevalent in business, health care, and public policy work. Turbulent environments, rapidly changing technologies, and increasingly specialized knowledge are some of the factors that are making collaboration more attractive to professors and society in general.

How Do Faculty Collaborate?

Fundamentally, faculty collaboration takes two principal forms—collaboration in research and collaboration in teaching. Considerable variation occurs within these two categories, however. Collaboration in research can vary on several dimensions, including its purpose, organizational structure, team composition, and duration. In "supplementary collaboration," for example, researchers divide tasks among distinctively qualified specialists and make separate contributions to a shared project. In "complementary collaboration," on the other hand, researchers with similar interests and qualifications work closely on all aspects of a joint endeavor (Smart and Bayer 1986).

Collaboration in teaching can differ along several dimensions as well. Various classification schemes divide team teaching according to the roles teachers play (specialist versus generalist, for example), the degree of hierarchy in the team structure (hierarchical versus interactive, for example), and the extent to which disciplinary perspectives are integrated or maintained as distinct in the teaching collaboration (Easterby-Smith and Olve 1984; Rinn and Weir 1984).

Collaborative practices differ considerably across fields. Collaboration is most common in "data disciplines" with development of strong paradigms (like physics or chemistry). Collaboration is less widely practiced in "word disciplines" (like sociology or political science) and is rare indeed in fields like philosophy or literature (Bayer and Smart 1988; Berelson 1960; Fox and Faver 1984).

What Are the Key Steps in Collaboration?
Although each collaborative arrangement is distinctive, collaboration generally follows a common pattern. Small-group theory helps to illuminate the dynamics of collaboration. For example, negotiated order theory (Gray 1989) sees collaboration as a process of negotiation among stake holders. This theory emphasizes the temporary and emergent nature of collaboration as participants work out the details of executing a shared project or activity. Although small-group models might label the steps in the collaborative process somewhat differently, each effective collaborative team must proceed through four basic stages: (1) choosing colleagues or team members, (2) dividing the labor, (3) establishing work guidelines, and (4) terminating a collaboration. The way collaborators execute each step influences the evolution and outcomes of the team's effort.

Why Is Faculty Collaboration Controversial?

Collaboration among faculty often raises issues of power, influence, professional identity, and integrity. Evaluating individual contributions to collaborative endeavors and allocating credit fairly among partners are difficult challenges that frequently plague collaborators. Exploitation of lower-status parties in collaborative groups (women, minorities, junior colleagues, students, for example) is another problem that sometimes results when academics pool their talents. Most professional societies and higher education institutions have not implemented policies for resolving complex problems that can result from teamwork. As collaboration becomes more standard in the academic profession, clear policies are needed to ensure that faculty derive the maximum benefit from working together.

What Recommendations Emerge from a Study of Collaboration among Faculty?

The growing trend toward collaboration has implications for faculty, administrators, and the general higher education community. Faculty who are accustomed to working alone should consider developing collaborative relationships. Carefully managed collaborative partnerships can enrich academic life. To be successful, collaborators must know the dynamics of the collaboration process and be prepared to cope with collaboration's challenges as well as reap its rewards.

Administrators have a key role to play in fostering effective collaboration. They can allocate discretionary resources and shape supportive policies to encourage faculty to work together. More important, administrators can stimulate collaborative work by recognizing and rewarding collaborative achievements in public and private ways. They can also promote teamwork by collaborating themselves in team teaching an occasional course or conducting research with faculty colleagues.

At present, many informal traditions and explicit policies (criteria for tenure and promotion, policies for merit pay, standards for faculty evaluation, for example) inhibit collaboration by faculty. If the higher education community wishes to encourage more faculty teamwork, some significant reforms will be needed. For example, as part of professional socialization, students should be introduced to the merits and processes of collaboration. Certainly, the frequently accepted idea that single-author publications are inherently more valuable than co-authored work should be reexamined. Breaking down the barriers that discourage collaboration by faculty is probably the most needed reform. By implementing supportive policies and creating organizational structures to facilitate collaboration across disciplinary and institutional boundaries, higher education could better reap the range of benefits that faculty collaboration promises.

What Questions Remain to Be Explored?
Many questions concerning faculty collaboration invite attention. Research that explores more deeply how the collaboration experience varies by discipline, type of institution, and career stage is needed. Studies specifically comparing the collaboration practices of genders and various ethnic groups would also enhance understanding of this complex phenomenon. More systematic research on the outcomes and benefits of collaboration is essential as well. Carefully crafted studies using qualitative and quantitative methodologies will help to eliminate myths about collaboration and enable faculty members to enter collaborative relationships armed with knowledge that will enhance their opportunities for a successful experience.

ADVISORY BOARD

CONSULTING EDITORS

A. Nancy Avakian
Metropolitan State University

Paula Y. Bagasao
University of California System

Rose R. Bell
New School for Social Research

David G. Brown
University of North Carolina-Asheville

Clifton F. Conrad
University of Wisconsin-Madison

James Cooper
FIPSE College Teaching Project

Richard A. Couto
Tennessee State University

John W. Creswell
University of Nebraska-Lincoln

Donald F. Dansereau
Texas Christian University

Peter Frederick
Wabash College

Virginia N. Gordon
Ohio State University

Wesley R. Habley
American College Testing

Michael L. Hanes
West Chester University

Dianne Horgan
Memphis State University

John L. Howarth
Private Consultant

Joan Isenberg
George Mason University

Susan Jeffords
University of Washington

REVIEW PANEL

Charles Adams
University of Massachusetts–Amherst

Louis Albert
American Association for Higher Education

Richard Alfred
University of Michigan

Philip G. Altbach
State University of New York–Buffalo

Marilyn J. Amey
University of Kansas

Louis C. Attinasi, Jr.
University of Houston

Robert J. Barak
Iowa State Board of Regents

Alan Bayer
Virginia Polytechnic Institute and State University

John P. Bean
Indiana University

Louis W. Bender
Florida State University

John M. Braxton
Syracuse University

Peter McE. Buchanan
Council for Advancement and
    Support of Education

John A. Centra
Syracuse University

Arthur W. Chickering
George Mason University

Shirley M. Clark
Oregon State System of Higher Education

Darrel A. Clowes
Virginia Polytechnic Institute and State University

John W. Creswell
University of Nebraska–Lincoln

Deborah DiCroce
Piedmont Virginia Community College

CONTENTS

FOREWORD

While a few of the disciplines value collaborative efforts, many, if not most, see collaborative teaching and research as less valid or less respectable than individual faculty efforts. These disciplines generally develop a viewpoint that focuses on the negative aspects of collaborative efforts. This negative paradigm, which many faculty developed from their own experiences as students, sees collaborative scholarship as manipulative or exploitive, with one or more of the parties involved getting credit for someone else's work. While this situation is always a possibility when people cooperate in an activity, the benefits of collaboration, on the whole, far outweigh the possible negative consequences. Each of the following four benefits of collaborative learning contributes in its own way to increased quality and productivity:

Greater intellectual creativity. It is a universally accepted principle in business and industry that the more minds working on a problem, the greater the chance of finding a solution. Researchers of high achievers from Napoleon Hill to Stephen Covey identify the characteristic of working in teams as a major trait of people who repeatedly effect successful outcomes. The success of the space program in the 1960s would never have occurred without the collaborative efforts of many different intellectual areas.

Higher productivity through mutual goals. For the collaborative process to work, a clear understanding of what the problem or activity is, who is going to do what, and when each of the parties will complete his or her responsibilities must be present. The more this division of effort is delineated, the greater the need within each individual to produce good-quality work in a timely way, lest they look bad to their colleagues. This incentive to produce can be very exciting and stimulating as the results of each party's efforts become part of the greater whole.

An atmosphere for mentoring and role modeling. One of the key elements of professionalization in medicine is that of role modeling from many mentors. In the disciplines, it is more the norm to promote scholarship with little or no assistance or to limit students to one mentor—usually the chair of the student's dissertation committee. This practice of scholarship in isolation is perpetuated as entering faculty members struggle without guidance to develop their courses and meet the publishing requirement necessary to achieve tenure. Involving senior faculty, junior faculty, and students together in collaborative teaching and research could greatly enhance the skills and professionalization of all concerned.

Appreciation and recognition for achievement. In an academic career, it is not unusual for a person to achieve the height of his or her profession by the mid-40s and have nothing but the same activities to look forward to for the remainder of the career. Because of the protective cloak of tenure and academic freedom, many academic leaders ignore the activities and the resulting accomplishments of their faculty, as they tend to matters they have more control over. This benign neglect often results in a feeling by the faculty of not being appreciated—a major reason for faculty members' dissatisfaction. When tough economic times eliminate other evidence of appreciation—funds for travel, teaching/ research assistance, and secretarial services, for example— this feeling is furthered magnified. The process of collaborative efforts automatically helps to reinforce the worth of each participant and creates an atmosphere of appreciation.

In this monograph, authors Ann E. Austin, associate professor in the Higher, Adult, and Lifelong Education Program at Michigan State University, and Roger G. Baldwin, associate professor of higher education at the College of William and Mary, synthesize the research and literature on collaboration in academic life. They review trends in collaboration and practices in different disciplinary fields of higher education and in other sectors. Their report recognizes the distinctive nature of various modes of collaboration, examines the generic elements of the collaboration process in detail, and examines such difficult topics as the fair awarding of credit for authorship and collaboration among colleagues of different status. The monograph concludes with recommendations for policy and practice, identifying questions that warrant further research.

Collaboration among faculty, when used to further the vision and mission of the institution or discipline, can greatly enhance the quality of scholarship and teaching. Academic leaders and faculty together need to learn to value collaborative activity as an important ingredient for ensuring the vitality of academe.

Jonathan D. Fife
Series Editor, Professor and
Director, ERIC Clearinghouse on Higher Education

PREFACE

This book consolidates research and writing from a variety
of fields to enhance understanding of faculty collaboration.
By reviewing and integrating this diverse body of literature,
we have each acquired an enhanced appreciation for effective
collaborative arrangements. We also have developed an im-
proved awareness of the myriad of factors that contribute to
the success or failure of faculty partnerships.

In addition to other sources of information, our own collaboration on this book has enhanced our knowledge of the
collaborative process. Similar to many collaborations, our
work together began informally once we discovered shared
professional interests. Smaller joint projects preceded our
decision to cooperate on a task of this magnitude. In this
book, each of us took principal responsibility for certain portions of the text. We worked out the overall plan together
and contributed ideas and advice on one another's sections,
however. The final manuscript is genuinely a shared product
to which we have each contributed an equal measure. Neither
of us could have written this book alone. It did not take shape
in our individual minds but through many conversations we
had about the topic over a long period of time. Like other
long-distance collaborations, we worked on the book whenever we could. We met to discuss it in Atlanta, San Francisco,
Washington, D.C., Nashville, and East Lansing. Each time we
gained additional insights, and the project moved along a
little farther. This lengthy process has taught us a great deal
about the difficulties and the considerable benefits of working
closely with colleagues on topics of mutual concern. We have
each gained respect for collaboration. Our professional lives
have been enriched by the process. And we will probably
be working together again soon. We hope this report will
entice its readers to give collaboration a try. As we discovered,
first-hand experience with collaboration is the best way to
learn about it.

Ann E. Austin
Roger G. Baldwin
February 1992

COLLABORATION IN ACADEMIC LIFE

Collaboration in the academic profession is a growing and controversial phenomenon. And it is an issue that deserves the careful attention of higher education and its leaders. The author of the best-selling book, *A Brief History of Time: From the Big Bang to Black Holes,* credits much of his success in theoretical physics to collaborators in successive phases of his intellectual odyssey, acknowledging both the physical and theoretical help he has received from colleagues and students. "Having to keep up with my students has been a great stimulation, and has . . . prevented me from getting stuck in a rut" (Hawking 1988, p. vii). Those collaborators have enabled him to continue the life of the mind despite the effects of a debilitating motor neuron condition, commonly known as Lou Gehrig's disease. This case, while extreme, clearly highlights the empowering capacity of collaborative relationships. Two or more people working cooperatively can do many things one person cannot do alone.

In contrast, scholarly collaboration can also be controversial. The 1989 Nobel prize in medicine was awarded to two American researchers without acknowledging the contribution of the French scientist who "performed the critical experiments for which his American professors won the award" (*Washington Post* 11 October 1989). "Controversies have frequently arisen over the Nobel science prizes, which single out a few individual researchers for special recognition in fields where new knowledge usually comes from the cooperative efforts of many scientists, students, and technicians."

An "intellectual sea change" (Boyer 1990, p. 21) could be under way within the academic profession. "Today, more than at any time in recent memory, researchers feel the need to move beyond traditional disciplinary boundaries, communicate with colleagues in other fields, and discover patterns that connect" (p. 20). The increasing frequency of faculty collaboration supports this assertion. The growth of collaboration could be part of a major redefinition of academic roles and the way they are carried out.

An expanded vision of scholarship is necessary if this country's higher education institutions are to remain vital and to keep pace with society's rapidly changing needs. Including teaching and efforts to integrate and apply knowledge as well as the discovery of knowledge into this revised definition of scholarship calls into question the conventional model of faculty practice. Any reassessment of scholarship and academic

The growth of collaboration could be part of a major redefinition of academic roles and the way they are carried out.

life generally must devote attention to the phenomenon of collaboration among faculty. Ignoring the collaborative dimension now common in academe would overlook "new realities both within the academy and beyond" (Boyer 1990, p. 3).

This monograph takes an in-depth look at collaboration in the academic profession. Its purpose is to enhance understanding of this growing trend by examining the forces that encourage professors to collaborate and reviewing the collaboration process. It also identifies the consequences, positive and negative, of collaborative activity and examines both the beneficial outcomes and the controversies surrounding collaboration. The monograph provides a foundation for the development of policies and procedures to foster and regulate the various forms of collaboration now common on college and university campuses. Finally, it identifies some of the questions and issues pertaining to collaboration that invite scholarly research. Though collaboration is an important part of work in academe, it has received surprisingly little attention from those who study faculty and their careers.

A Growing Phenomenon

In many fields of study, the image of the solitary scholar working alone in a library carrel or laboratory is no more than a fond memory or historic artifact. Forty years ago, a writer suggested that "the modern Charles Darwin" would not be found working privately in a library or on lone travels to the Galapagos Islands (Eaton 1951). Rather, he would most likely be a member of the staff of a large university or research institute, where he would integrate his work with any number of collaborators. Products of major collaborative efforts are now so common in our society that it is difficult to imagine life without them. Microwave ovens, color television, and the modern computer resulted from highly trained specialists pooling their resources to unleash creativity no one possessed by himself.

"In the strongholds of research, the isolated rooms in the ivory tower may not be the best habitat for achievement" (Pelz and Andrews 1966, p. 237). This view holds that complete autonomy can be debilitating to a member of the academic profession. It isolates individuals from stimulation offered by colleagues and leaves them confined by the limits of their own knowledge and imagination.

In contrast to the classical image of the scholar, the modern academic works closely with colleagues in teaching and research. Team teaching and collaborative research are now common in many fields of study. Collaborative scholarship has grown exponentially since World War II (see, e.g., Baum et al. 1976; Bayer and Smart 1988; Beaver and Rosen 1978, 1979; Fox and Faver 1984; Over 1982; Patel 1973), and collaboration among academics is not a new phenomenon (Beaver and Rosen 1978, 1979). Collaboration clearly has become more common in recent decades, however, as the funding and methodology of research have changed (Beaver and Rosen 1979). In the first decade of this century, for example, 75 percent of publications in the biological and physical sciences had only one author. Between 1950 and 1959, however, single authorship in those fields dropped to 19 percent (Zuckerman and Merton 1972). The field of psychology exhibits a similar trend. Single-author publications declined from almost 66 percent in 1949 to under 33 percent in 1979 (Over 1982). During the same period, the mean number of authors per article in journals of the American Psychological Association increased from 1.47 to 2.19 (Over 1982). An even more complex process could be under way (Patel 1973). In addition to the trend from single to multiple authorship is a trend from a single institutional base of authorship to cross-institutional collaboration. Essentially, academics are moving from a mode of self-reliance to a mode of multipurpose assistance.

These trends have both positive and negative implications. Collaboration has enlivened many classrooms and led to numerous products that have enriched our lives. Many academics have been rejuvenated by the opportunity to work closely with younger colleagues or peers who bring different disciplinary perspectives to a teaching or research problem. Yet collaboration also poses serious problems for higher education. Fair distribution of credit for co-authored work is a significant concern on some college campuses. Likewise, administrators and faculty colleagues often have difficulty evaluating the products of collaborative research or teaching. Complex ethical questions arise when senior academics take advantage of their junior colleagues or individuals are listed as authors of works to which they contributed very little of substance.

Today collaboration is clearly a fact of academic life. More and more professors teach cooperatively. Many also conduct research in tandem with others and co-author articles and books. Yet higher education has not completely acknowledged or accepted this phenomenon. Remarkably little research and writing analyze the process of academic collaboration, and scarcely a handful of universities and professional organizations have developed systematic policies for regulating and evaluating collaborative practices and products. For these reasons, a comprehensive survey of the research and literature on faculty collaboration is overdue. To respond appropriately to a growing trend, colleges and universities must look carefully at the many forms of collaboration that now occupy a large portion of professors' time and energy.

Definition

To proceed with this analysis, it is essential to define "collaboration." Regrettably, it is not an easy task. Even within the boundaries of higher education, collaboration means different things to different people. To collaborate is to work in combination toward a unified action (Cameron 1984). Or collaboration is laboring with others, cooperating, working as part of a team, and it involves blending oneself into a group to move effectively together (Keohane 1985). Or collaboration is a process of functional interdependence in an attempt to coordinate skills, tools, and rewards (Patel 1973).

It is important to distinguish collaboration from cooperation, especially because the two are sometimes used interchangeably. Collaboration is the narrower term. Collaboration requires a great deal of cooperation, but the final objectives of the two activities differ somewhat. Individuals who cooperate often reach some agreements but proceed individually toward self-determined goals (Hord 1981). In contrast, people who collaborate work closely together and share mutual responsibility for their joint endeavor. According to this conceptualization, collaboration not only involves cooperative action. It emerges from shared goals and leads to outcomes that benefit all partners.

As this monograph makes clear, collaboration comes in many forms. What constitutes collaboration in one academic setting might not be typical in another. The organization and sharing of work for one collaborative team can differ from the way in which another group divides and accomplishes its work. Hence, no definition of collaboration is comprehensive or completely satisfying. Collaboration might be one of

those words, like "salad" or "game," that is essentially unde-
finable but can be understood by looking at the characteristics
with which it is often associated (Whipple 1987). The tongue-
in-cheek question, "Is a bowl of gazpacho, served before a
main course, a salad?" (p. 4), helps to illustrate the difficulty
of defining collaboration. But although the outer limits of a
concept like collaboration are fuzzy, the term is well enough
understood to be useful.

For the purposes of this monograph, faculty collaboration
is described as a cooperative endeavor that involves common
goals, coordinated effort, and outcomes or products for which
the collaborators share responsibility and credit. This descrip-
tion is intentionally broad and flexible because it must accom-
modate collaboration in both research and teaching in different disciplines and different types of institutions in our
complex higher education system.

Why Academics Collaborate

The reasons for the significant growth of collaboration in the
academic profession are complex. The ultimate rationale for
collaboration "is for the participants to make use of each
others' talents to do what they either could not have done
at all or as well alone" (Wildavsky 1986, p. 237). This reason-
ing is valid on the face, but it tells us little about why collaboration has become increasingly common throughout the academic ranks. Several forces, both social and psychological,
seem to be encouraging more and more professors to work
closely with their colleagues (Gibson 1987). "Accelerating
demands to publish have fanned the fires of more than a few
mutual efforts" (p. 56). Further, the logistics of large-scale
research necessitate collaboration by academics in many
fields. The complex issues facing society and educators today partially account for the growth of team teaching. Many
faculty trained in specialized subject fields feel ill-prepared
to teach by themselves courses that require an interdisciplinary perspective.

The forces promoting collaboration can be divided into
two categories, organizational/institutional factors and individual factors (Fox and Faver 1982). At the organizational level
are the increased availability of student assistants, technical personnel, and electronic equipment, and the increased support
for research on a grand scale (Patel 1973). Certainly, the latest
generation of communications technology facilitates collab-

oration, especially over long distances. Facsimile machines, electronic mail, word-processing systems, and telephone answering machines make the logistics of working collaboratively on scholarship and teaching less cumbersome and quicker than was the case previously. Further, the maturation of the disciplines and increasingly specialized research technology help to account for the growth of collaboration (Fox and Faver 1984). The emergence of conceptual models and theoretical paradigms in many fields helps specialists to divide the labor in their quest for new knowledge. Similarly, a team of faculty working collaboratively can bring their individual areas of expertise to the teaching of a course that covers an array of topics, thereby enhancing their students' educational experience. Today, scholars cannot operate by themselves the state-of-the-art equipment now in use in many fields. Likewise, individual researchers, or even individual institutions, cannot afford to shoulder the expense of the sophisticated facilities necessary for research and teaching on the cutting edge in some disciplines. For many academics, collaboration has become less an option than a requirement for success.

Indeed, much collaboration can be attributed to the increased professionalization of science (Beaver and Rosen 1978). Collaboration has become a mechanism for gaining recognition in the professional/academic community. It "provides a means of demonstrating one's ability to those in a position to 'recognize' others as well as [a means for] keeping up one's output from such a position" (p. 69). The nature of the scholarly enterprise has changed dramatically in recent decades, requiring, in many cases, more sophisticated approaches to instruction and research. A well-conceived collaborative arrangement eases access to the special expertise, skills, and facilities professors need to succeed in today's academic environment (Beaver and Rosen 1978). It appears that both organizational and related professional variables are stimulating the increase of collaboration in academe.

A variety of individual factors ＇ fostering more collaboration as well. The des e professional isolation and maintain motivation ompetitive environment is encouraging profe out to their colleagues (Fox and Faver 1982). Elementary social psychology explains that individuals are more likely to follow through on projects that involve commitments to others than projects with no external accountability. By joining their resources and dividing labor, academics can increase their productivity and attain goals that would be unreachable if they worked independently.

Professors who collaborate in teaching or scholarship assume that they will reap a variety of benefits from the effort they expend cooperatively. In addition to greater productivity, enhanced quality and increased risk-taking are often associated with collaborative arrangements (Fox and Faver 1984). It is widely assumed that better, and perhaps more original, ideas are likely to emerge when two or more people put their heads together. A socially reinforcing work group not only has the potential to foster creativity, but can also provide the security academics need to challenge conventional thinking and standard practices in their discipline or profession.

Collaboration with colleagues can unleash simple yet powerful forces (equally pertinent to female *and* male collaborators today):

> . . . one way . . . is by providing new ideas—jostling a man out of his old ways of thinking about things. . . . Then there is the possibility of a colleague catching an error [that] the man himself is too engrossed to see. . . . Still another way colleague contacts [can] help a person is in keeping him on his toes—simple things, like putting in a good day's work, or running a test the way it should be done . . . (Pelz and Andrews 1966, p. 52).

In short, collaboration offers a source of support for improving performance, maximizing potential, and achieving the goals that attracted many to the academic profession.

Academic Life: A Social Process

Research and productivity in our society are generally seen as the outcome of individual initiative rather than the results of a fertile environment that combines the talent and energy of two or more individuals (Nobel 1986). The Anglo-American tradition of research views its past achievements primarily in terms of the "lone wolf," the great individual, or the hero of science (Beaver and Rosen 1978). We often hold a "cherished image of the artist as solitary creator" and regard the idea of artistic collaboration as a surprising conception (McCabe 1984, p. 15). Even the role of teacher, though by definition a communal activity, is commonly understood as highly autonomous, with the individual in complete control and totally responsible for the success or failure of what goes on in the classroom.

In modern business and industry, the spirit of rugged individualism is dying out of necessity (Shreeve et al. 1986). And a somewhat similar pattern has begun to emerge within the academic profession. Contrary to the popular view, academics are social beings, and much academic work is done in groups, partnerships, or teams. Some theorists now even argue that the very act of knowing or knowledge construction is a social process. Academics develop understanding and discover new knowledge through a process of continual conversation and negotiation (Bruffee 1984). According to this perspective, even in the "hard" sciences, knowledge is a social artifact rather than totally objective, indisputable fact (Kuhn 1970). Within this framework, teaching and learning are best understood as collaborative activities. Similarly, scholarship typically is, to a great degree, collaborative as well.

Research documents that collegial communication and collaboration are closely associated with professional productivity. Social connectedness with colleagues is positively related to productivity in publication among natural scientists (Finkelstein 1984). One of the key environmental factors that mediates the level of productivity is collegial exchange and communication (Fox 1985a). "Data indicate that collegial exchange stimulates research involvement by testing ideas, activating interests, and reinforcing work" (p. 266). The highest-performing academics in numerous fields often begin to collaborate early, usually during graduate school (Finkelstein 1984), and they maintain this pattern of work throughout their professional lives. Empirical evidence indicates that high-performing academics are also among their fields' most active collaborators (Bayer and Smart 1988). Similarly, in some cases, scientists who performed at the highest levels spent considerably more time in communication with colleagues than their less productive peers (Pelz and Andrews 1966).

Even though collaboration is becoming more common within the academic ranks, it is by no means a uniform phenomenon. It varies by disciplinary field, by gender, and according to a host of other factors. In addition, academics employ many different forms of collaboration, some more successfully than others.

A close examination of current collaborative practice among professors raises an array of questions about this growing phenomenon. Yet no comprehensive survey of collaboration in the academic profession currently exists. The literature on collaboration is widely dispersed and difficult to access. Moreover, it tends to be atheoretical. Descriptions of collaborative practice are available for various fields, but most of these reports give little insight into the common attributes or the complexities that characterize collaboration across the board. Even fewer publications address the implications of collaboration for policy and practice in the higher education community.

The mystery surrounding successful collaborative arrangements must be solved. Some myths need to be laid to rest and many questions answered. The following sections present a comprehensive overview of the literature and research currently available on collaboration in academic life, and the monograph provides a conceptual context for understanding current collaborative practice and for considering how to capitalize on the potential collaboration offers to the academic profession. The following pages attempt to answer these questions:

The mystery surrounding successful collaborative arrangements must be solved.

1. What forms of collaboration are practiced in the academic profession?
2. Do the collaboration practices of academics differ by discipline, by gender, or according to other variables?
3. What theories or conceptual perspectives help illuminate the structure and process of collaboration among faculty members?
4. What are the basic steps in the collaborative process?
5. What problems and ethical questions commonly surround collaborative efforts?
6. What factors promote and what factors inhibit collaboration among professors?
7. How can institutional policies and administrative leadership optimize the advantages of collaborative work?
8. What are the most pressing questions regarding faculty collaboration that researchers could fruitfully address?

THE TREND TOWARD COLLABORATION

Collaboration is a trend gaining momentum in U.S. society. The terms used might vary across sectors—cooperative work, quality circles, teamwork, joint projects, group work—as might the particular forms of collaboration. Nevertheless, an array of factors are causing workers, managers, teachers, students, citizen groups, and others to consider seriously the benefits of working cooperatively to achieve important goals. "Team building is in" (George 1987, p. 122).

The wide and growing interest in teamwork and collaboration is evidenced in the many recently published books pertaining to the topic (see, e.g., Kanter 1983; Lawler 1986; Peters 1987). Seminars, retreats, and consultants are readily available for those wishing to learn more about the benefits, forms, and processes of collaboration and how they could use it in their own work.

This section presents a brief overview of some of the collaborative practices developing in other sectors, specifically highlighting the trend toward teamwork in the business sector and the growing interest in collaborative learning at all levels of education. It also notes a variety of other parts of our society where teamwork is used. While the focus of this monograph is the specific forms of collaboration in which faculty engage, an understanding of faculty collaboration—its benefits and pitfalls, its forms, and the steps through which collaborative relationships are forged—is deepened by an awareness of the broader context surrounding this dimension of faculty work. Some of the factors that encourage teamwork in the business world, in elementary, secondary, or college classrooms, or in the health arena also lead faculty members to consider sharing work with colleagues. Some of what we have learned about how small groups typically initiate, develop, negotiate, and complete their work is informed by research on teamwork and collaboration in other sectors. Faculty collaboration cannot be fully understood if it is seen as an unusual and atypical form of work rather than as one form of what is becoming a more general trend in our society.

Teamwork in the Business Sector

Historically, U.S. culture has embraced individual entrepreneurism, autonomy, and independence. But evidence is mounting that this "pioneering metaphor" is giving way, to some extent, to a new metaphor that emphasizes interdependence and complementarity (Gray 1989, pp. 269–70). A number of forces are converging in business and industry to heighten interest in collaboration and teamwork, a leading one of which is the increasing turbulence and complexity of the environment. The marketplace is widening and competition becoming more intense. Fast-paced technological change is another factor leading to collaboration, as U.S. companies wishing to stay on the cutting edge seek to use the expertise, ideas, and talents of an array of different people and must find ways to bring the knowledge of these people together quickly and efficiently. Linked to the fast pace of technological change is the press for shorter periods between development and introduction of new products. A competitive stance can be maintained only if new ideas are translated quickly into new or updated products. Innovation and speed are not the only challenges, however; they must be coupled with the cost-effectiveness necessitated by a tight, competitive economy and the high standards of quality demanded by knowledgeable consumers prepared to give their business to those companies whose products are perceived to be strongest. In the face of these intertwining factors, U.S. industry is recognizing that teamwork and collaboration in a variety of forms provide useful and productive outcomes (Gray 1989; Parker 1990).

Those who use or have worked with teams in the business sector cite a variety of benefits (Gray 1989; Parker 1990). Teams can increase productivity in several ways. When members of different parts of the development, production, and sales forces communicate regularly, redundancy can be reduced and resources used more wisely. Furthermore, teamwork promotes trust and communication, thus freeing more human energy from typical political concerns to the resolution of issues specifically related to the work and the product. The use of teams also promotes innovation and creativity by bringing the ideas of more than one person to the task. In addition to these benefits of greater productivity and efficiency, heightened creativity and quality, and enhanced competitiveness, teamwork is usually enjoyable for the members (Parker 1990). Personal satisfaction grows as individuals share ideas, take responsibility for a challenging task, and interact with others. As our society increasingly emphasizes the importance of quality of work life, this benefit remains significant (Parker 1990). As discussed later, many of these benefits are similar to those that attract faculty members to collaboration.

Collaboration in business and industry occurs in a variety of ways and across diverse groups. One type of teamwork occurs when a company seeks to enhance innovation, productivity, and quality by bringing together employees from various functional areas. The usual strategy of using task forces and committees is widening to include quality circles (groups of workers at similar levels who discuss and identify ways to improve quality) and self-managing work teams (responsible for setting their own pace, allocating responsibilities, and maintaining quality control) (Parker 1990). Such companies as AT&T and NCR Corporation use "concurrent engineering," whereby all those connected to a product work simultaneously rather than sequentially. In this approach, the design engineers, the production workers, and the sales staff all work at the same time on their aspect of product development and communicate regularly about progress and problems. Those using this form of collaboration report that a project can be completed in about half the usual time and that last-minute difficulties are less likely than with sequential work (Port, Schiller, and King 1990). Each form of teamwork within companies involves flexible work structures and wider participation by employees in management of the work and workplace.

Among the other types of collaboration in the business sector are the alliances that emerge among various groups associated with particular industries. Management, workers, labor unions, distributors, and communities are engaging in joint planning and decision making with the view that the success of the industry has important implications for an array of constituencies. One example of this form of collaboration is the new General Motors Saturn plant in Tennessee. Another example is the cooperative effort between management and labor that increasingly occurs in a number of industries to save jobs, often in reaction to economic decline, increased competition, and other environmental turbulence. This kind of teamwork is evidenced by joint labor-management committees on the work site, dialogue between regional and national union and management leadership, sweeping redesign of the workplace, and alternative reward systems like gain-sharing and profit-sharing plans (Gray 1989; Parker 1990).

Collaboration across companies within an industry is also happening. International joint ventures contribute to innovation by enabling several companies to share the cost of developing and investing in new technology. Companies also enter these ventures for the purposes of expanding their technological knowledge, using a country's own company to help another company enter a foreign market, and trading technological, design, or production secrets (Gray 1989; Hamel, Doz, and Prahalad 1989). Telecommunication, computer, robotic, and automobile industries have all engaged in international joint ventures.

A fourth type of collaboration in the business sector is the teaming between government, business, and often labor. The government's involvement in business matters is increasing, while, at the same time, companies influence the government by lobbying and bringing up various social and political issues. Joint effort and collaboration often result from recognition that the same issues confront both sectors.

This brief review of teamwork in business and industry assists the study of faculty collaboration. While these forms of collaboration differ in significant ways from collaboration in higher education, they emerge for some of the same reasons that lead members of the professoriate to find collaboration inviting. "Theory, Structure, and Process of Collaboration," later in this monograph, draws on research concerning teams in business and industry to enhance the understanding of collaboration among faculty.

Collaborative Learning

In elementary and secondary classrooms, and to some extent in university and college classrooms, students participate in collaborative learning experiences. Peer response groups, small-group projects, long-term study teams, and collaborative writing groups are among the variety of team experiences students might encounter. The American Association for Higher Education's Action Community on Collaborative Learning defines this form of cooperation in higher education as follows:

> *Collaboration in undergraduate education is a pedagogical style that emphasizes cooperative efforts among students, faculty, and administrators. Rooted in the belief that learning is inherently social in nature, it stresses common inquiry as the basic learning process* (cited in Whipple 1987, p. 3).

A key element in collaborative learning is its epistemological perspective that knowledge is socially constructed, created by communities rather than individuals. Many disciplines embrace social constructionism, which asserts that, as a social construct, knowledge belongs to and emerges from communities. That is, through their conversations and interactions, and in the context of particular and changing political and social environments, communities of individuals create and shape knowledge. Knowledge is not transmitted or poured into students but rather emerges from the ongoing dialogue and social interaction within groups. Knowledge created in this way is more than the compilation or summation of each individual's knowledge (Bruffee 1986, 1987; MacGregor 1990; Whipple 1987).

Several philosophical and educational roots contribute to current thinking on collaborative learning (MacGregor 1990). The work of Dewey and Piaget on the benefits of experiential learning and of student-centered instruction and research in social psychology on the small-group process has been a primary influence on the development of this form of pedagogy. Additionally, feminist theory and pedagogy inform proponents of collaborative learning. Feminist theory advances similar epistemological assumptions as the collaborative learning movement, emphasizing that learning occurs as individuals interact with each other in the process of engaging the material; learning is not a process of being filled like an empty vessel (Belenky et al. 1986).

A variety of programs in higher education (both historical and current) also contribute to the collaborative learning movement (MacGregor 1990). Historically, the experimental colleges of the 1920s as well as those of the 1960s were efforts to reorganize the college curriculum to foster more intellectual engagement by students. The Great Books programs have had similar goals. More recently, efforts in several disciplines have both drawn on and contributed to collaborative learning. Kenneth Bruffee of the City University of New York, for example, is well known for his use of peer writing groups to develop students' writing and thinking skills. Uri Triesman of the University of Texas has been sharing his experiences in using student collaboration to teach college math.

A variety of characteristics distinguish collaborative learning. First, collaborative learning involves positive interdependence among group members, with each feeling a responsibility for the group and its task (Cooper and Mueck 1990; MacGregor 1990). Proponents of the particular form of collaboration called "cooperative learning" emphasize that all group members take responsibility to ensure that each member learns (Johnson, Johnson, and Smith 1991a, 1991b). Additionally, cooperative learning involves individual accountability achieved through having each person's grade calculated on the basis of both individual and group work. A second feature of collaborative learning is that it encourages students to learn the social skills necessary for cooperation, such as listening actively, offering effective criticism, and sharing their talents and abilities in ways that benefit the group (Cooper and Mueck 1990). Students also are encouraged to assume some of the authority traditionally residing with the instructor (Bruffee 1987). A third characteristic of collaborative learning is that it creates a sense of community. Teachers and students often become more closely engaged as they actively participate in the educational process. Students learn to help each other and, through collaboration, become more tolerant and respectful of individual differences (Cooper and Mueck 1990; MacGregor 1987; Whipple 1987). As discussed later, many of the characteristics of collaborative learning as students experience it parallel the experiences of faculty members whose collaborations enable them to work and learn together.

Collaborative learning in colleges and universities can take many forms. It can include, for example, small groups of students working together on a project, teams of two engaging in a short brainstorming session as part of a class, a small number of students reading and reacting to each other's drafts, and a long-standing group of students who meet regularly to review assignments and assist and monitor each other's learning (MacGregor 1990; Whipple 1987). Cooperative learning groups can be categorized as one of three types (Johnson, Johnson, and Smith 1991a, 1991b). *Formal cooperative learning groups,* typically comprised of two to six students, are formed for a period of time to accomplish a particular project or task, such as a report or presentation. *Informal cooperative learning groups* are less structured and exist for just a short time—groups of two or three to answer a question using material just presented in a lecture, for example. *Base groups* consist of groups of students who meet on a long-term basis to give peer support, share resources, and encourage each other in learning.

While the lack of systematic implementation of cooperative learning at the college level has mitigated against the development of a large body of knowledge about the impact of this form of teamwork on postsecondary students, studies at lower educational levels of the impact of cooperative learning are more numerous. A series of meta-analyses offers strong evidence of cooperation's strength—often surpassing traditional teaching methods—in promoting achievement and productivity (Johnson et al. 1981). This pattern held true for all subject areas and age groups tested. Minority and female students in particular have shown advances in achievement associated with cooperative learning (Cooper and Mueck 1990; Slavin 1983).

Other effects of cooperative learning include enhanced self-esteem and greater respect between participating students. For example, students with varying levels of academic ability and students from different ethnic groups develop more mutual respect and liking for each other. Additionally, students who participate in cooperative learning develop more positive attitudes toward school in general, become more competent and confident learners, gain in altruism, and grow in their appreciation of the benefits of cooperation (Slavin 1983). Proponents of collaborative learning in higher education argue that these results can be expected in higher education also (MacGregor 1987, 1990).

The Growing Interest in Collaboration

In addition to the business and industrial world and the undergraduate classroom, collaboration is increasing in a variety of other areas. The medical profession, for example, is recognizing the necessity of teamwork, as evidenced by the trend toward group practice and the teaming of physicians, social workers, and social service agencies. In some medical schools, students are required to work in collaborative groups (Bruffee 1987).

Collaboration also is increasing in the area of conflict resolution, where adversarial work is giving way to more negotiated and mediated settlements. In the political sector, individuals, agencies, and interest groups are more frequently looking to build partnerships. Serious societal concerns, such as environmental problems, homelessness, and crime prevention, are increasingly seen to require the cooperation and joint efforts of an array of interested citizens and groups. All in all, evidence is mounting that the complexity of today's pressing issues and challenges is eliciting more interest in collaboration and cooperation than in the past.

Faculty members in U.S. colleges and universities are affected by and part of this trend also. Many of the reasons that prompt collaboration in the business, political, or medical sectors—for example, the complexity of late 20th century challenges and the need to use a variety of areas of expertise in addressing problems—encourage faculty members to consider working with colleagues. Many faculty members are not strangers to collaboration, having used their roles as researchers and consultants to help in the establishment of some of the business practices discussed. Some faculty members, particularly those in the sciences, have worked with government and independent research agencies that foster large-scale collaborative work. The belief that collaboratively produced knowledge is greater than what an individual can produce alone—one of the assumptions undergirding collaborative learning—also undoubtedly motivates some faculty members to forgo some of their autonomy by joining others.

As this monograph shows throughout, faculty collaboration is its own form of work, quite distinct from other versions of teamwork. Yet an awareness of the broader context in which collaboration is developing in a number of sectors adds to the belief that faculty collaboration should be studied and encouraged. Furthermore, a look at collaboration in other sectors suggests questions and issues to consider in exploring collaboration among faculty members. Specifically, the forms, benefits, problems, and outcomes of collaboration vary across and within sectors. This monograph addresses these and other issues as they pertain to collaboration among faculty members in higher education.

COLLABORATION IN RESEARCH AND SCHOLARSHIP

Professors cannot be completely effective if they work continuously in isolation: Rather than being a solitary activity, the best scholarship brings faculty together and mutually reinforces their efforts in research and in teaching (Boyer 1990). Indeed, in an era confronted with complex social, technological, and economic problems, a team approach to many research and instructional tasks might not just be desirable; it might be *essential.*

Collaboration is not a uniform strategy that can be applied with equal effectiveness in a variety of academic settings, however. Collaboration among academics takes many forms. To enhance understanding of these diverse and sometimes complex arrangements, it is necessary to impose some order on the variety of ways professors work collaboratively. This section looks closely at collaboration in research; the next examines collaboration in teaching. Despite their common attributes, collaboration in research and in teaching are distinctly different processes. The literature on collaboration in research and in teaching also differs qualitatively. Much more information based on data is available on collaboration in research than on collaboration in teaching. The literature on team teaching, in contrast, tends to be more anecdotal and prescriptive.

Forms of Collaboration in Research

Collaboration in research covers a wide spectrum of activity. In the broadest sense, it ranges from contributing ideas and information to an ongoing research initiative to complete involvement in a research project and co-authoring publications with one or more other people (Begum and Sami 1988). Collaboration can be formal and highly structured—a working partnership with a clear division of labor, a fixed schedule of meetings, and clear deadlines, for example. Or it can be more casual and open ended—when colleagues jointly author a book over many years, for example (Tomlinson, Semradek, and Boyd 1986).

A distinction between "traditional" and "modern" teamwork is necessary (Hagstrom 1964). The dominant form of collaboration has changed with the evolution of various disciplines and new developments in the research enterprise. Traditional scientific teamwork consisted simply of freely collaborating scholars or teachers collaborating with their students. Typically, they began to work cooperatively when they discovered shared interests or when they realized their work required the assistance of others (Hagstrom 1964). Two sociologists working together on a study of the attitudes of residents of a local subsidized housing project is an example of this kind of traditional teamwork.

In contrast, modern teamwork is more complex and less spontaneous, and often occurs on a grander scale than earlier forms of collaboration. Multifaceted research problems sometimes require large numbers of people from different disciplines to work together. The Manhattan Project that secretly employed large numbers of scientists in the research that led to production of the first atomic bomb is perhaps the best known example of modern teamwork. Modern teamwork can involve a sharp division of labor, separation of the researcher from the tools of production, and greater centralization of authority (Hagstrom 1964). Both traditional and modern forms of teamwork exist on college and university campuses today. In some fields, the balance has shifted toward the latter, and a major debate on the merits of "big science" (major research projects involving sizable staffs, large budgets, and elaborate administrative structures) versus "little science" (a few scholars with a relatively small budget conducting hands-on research) is under way.

Collaboration can be consolidated into three generic categories: "complementary," "supplementary," and "master-apprentice" (Smart and Bayer 1986). Each form of collaboration occurs for distinctive reasons and represents a distinctive process. Likewise, each offers its own benefits and disadvantages.

In *complementary collaboration,* scholars come together out of a desire to avoid intellectual isolation. Rather than divide a project into pieces, they work on the same problem at the same time, hoping to overcome blocks that impede their intellectual progress (Hagstrom 1965). For example, two colleagues with a shared interest in academic career development engage in complementary collaboration when they agree to work together on a secondary analysis of existing data. By examining the same information in tandem, they provoke one another's thinking and arrive at original insights together that neither one could achieve independently. This type of collaboration is less formal. Often participants do not even officially agree to work together on a particular project. Rather, their informal communication gradually leads them into "successively greater commitments to cooperate" (Hagstrom 1965).

Collaborative research arrangements can be divided into four categories, Types A through D (Cohen, Kruse, and Anbar 1982). Type B teams are examples of complementary collaboration. This type of collaborative arrangement is highly participatory and decentralized. Members of Type B teams are jointly involved in the planning and implementation of research tasks. They engage in more give-and-take communication than do other types of research teams. Collaboration of this type is a true "collective activity involving mutual agreement and sharing of responsibility among team members" (p. 211).

Supplementary collaboration, on the other hand, typically occurs for a specific purpose. The goals of this type of collaborative effort cannot generally be achieved by a person working alone. Hence, the participants acknowledge a need to divide labor among experts who possess specialized knowledge and skills. Research requiring the involvement of survey design specialists, ethnographers, and statisticians to investigate the voting patterns of newly naturalized citizens is a form of supplementary collaboration. Scholars enter into this form of collaboration more consciously and more formally than they enter a complementary arrangement, delegating individual areas of responsibility. Collaboration involving a division of labor requires less a "meeting of minds" (Hagstrom 1965), hence less "courting" behavior to secure the cooperation of collaborators. This type of collaboration is less like a marriage, perhaps, and more like a business partnership.

Type C teamwork (Cohen, Kruse, and Anbar 1982) is akin to supplementary collaboration. Type C team members are a loose confederation of independent entrepreneurs. In this type of arrangement, each team member has a virtually independent subproject that involves only limited coordination with the work of the research partners. Supplementary collaborators are working toward essentially a common goal, but each has a distinctly different role to play as they move toward their mutual objective.

Master-apprentice collaboration typically involves a professor and one or more graduate students working on a common research topic. A microbiologist conducting research with the aid of graduate assistants who maintain bacterial cultures, run experiments, and analyze data is a classic example

Collaboration can be consolidated into three generic categories: "complementary," "supplementary," and "master apprentice."

of master-apprentice collaboration. This type of collaborative arrangement tends to be more hierarchical than the previous two arrangements. Authoritative direction is more likely when people do not share the same level of skill or status, especially when the collaborative experience is seen as part of the instructional process (Hagstrom 1965).

Type A teamwork (Cohen, Kruse, and Anbar 1982) parallels the master-apprentice model of collaboration, tending to be highly centralized and a one-person show. The veteran scholar who is clearly in charge is aided by subordinates who are still learning the craft of research.

In between the extremes of hierarchical and totally egalitarian collaboration is Type D teamwork, in which team members share rights in planning and setting research goals. In other words, the arrangement is participatory in intellectual matters, but it has a centralized administrative structure. The implementation of research plans, the assignment of tasks, and the supervision of activities are primarily the responsibilities of the principal investigator rather than a collective duty (Cohen, Kruse, and Anbar 1982).

The metaphor of the surgical team can be used to illustrate this form of collaboration. In this type of teamwork, the chief surgeon consults with colleagues about the patient's diagnosis and options for treatment, but "once the patient is on the table, the chief surgeon is unequivocally in charge" (Cohen, Kruse, and Anbar 1982, p. 212).

Action research is another form of collaboration in which faculty members might engage. This form of collaboration is designed to bring faculty members together with nonacademics for the purpose of improving practice or addressing a practical problem. For example, university faculty members in education, elementary and secondary teachers, and school staff development leaders might work together to find solutions to a particular problem confronting a public school. Similarly, a sociologist might collaborate with a citizens' group to analyze landownership and tax structures in a rural area (see Gaventa 1980). While collaborative action research focuses on exploring, addressing, or solving a societal problem, its results also usually contribute to the development of theory. When collaborative action research occurs in secondary or elementary classrooms and schools, professional development for participants is typically a third goal; collaborators gain new knowledge, experience new opportunities for collegiality, and might develop greater self-confidence (Oja and Smulyan 1989).

Subauthorship collaboration is a form of collaboration that is easily overlooked because it is less visible than other types of collaboration. Yet subauthorship collaboration has grown in the same way as multiple authorship (Patel 1973). Authors often acknowledge assistance others have provided in the preparation of their manuscripts. Data gathering and analysis, editing, and sharing research facilities are among the forms of help that subauthorship collaborators commonly provide. Frequently, the finished product could not have been produced without the help of others. Yet this form of collaboration is usually recognized only in the form of footnotes—if it is recognized at all.

Multiple Authorship

Collaborative writing, like other forms of collaboration, covers a spectrum of activity and cannot be defined as a specific activity or sequence (Brady 1988). Collaboration can occur at any point in the writing process; collaborative writing ranges from editorial contributions to full joint authorship, from master-apprentice collaboration to editor-author collaborations, and to peer collaborations. Three major forms of collaborative writing—editorial collaboration, partial collaboration, and whole or full collaboration—require different degrees of authority, agreement, dialogue, and negotiation to ensure that the shared writing project is successful (Brady 1988).

In *editorial collaboration,* one person authors a work and another person edits the work for publication. Editorial collaboration falls outside the operational definition of collaboration used in this monograph. It is a common form of cooperative scholarship and deserves mention, however. In this collaborative situation, the author and the editor are not true equals, because authority for a text rests primarily with one writer. Issues of negotiation and flexibility are less important than the editor's clear understanding of the writer's goals. Editorial collaboration is less complex than other forms of scholarly collaboration, because clear lines of authority prevent some of the awkward situations that partners in research must talk through to move ahead with their work (Brady 1988).

Partial collaboration and full collaboration in writing fall more precisely within this monograph's definition of collaboration. In *partial collaboration,* authors divide a writing assignment, and each takes responsibility for specific sections. Much like supplementary collaborators, partial collaborators distribute textual authority fairly evenly but maintain some autonomy in the areas they write. Negotiation is less important in partial collaboration than "sharing an overall textual goal and accommodating—rather than integrating—new ideas" (Brady 1988, p. 168).

Full collaboration is probably the purist and least common form of co-authorship. No clear division of labor or authority exists. Successful full collaboration, like complementary collaboration, relies heavily on consensus; hence, it requires a great deal of discussion and negotiation to ensure its success. "Nothing goes out of the house without the other person concurring that this is the way of presenting it. . . . [We] achieve consensus on, literally, every word" (Brady 1988, p. 169).

Partial collaboration is the more common type of co-authorship. The intense interpersonal and time demands of full collaboration make it quite rare. Seldom do two or more authors have time to discuss every aspect of their writing project or critique every draft of the text (Brady 1988). More typically, co-authors agree to relinquish some of their authority at some point in the process. Alternatively, they defer to considerations of genre or professional conventions to resolve differences of opinion about their shared project.

Variation across Academic Fields
Collaboration varies substantially across academic fields as well. It is practically standard practice in some disciplines; in others, it is a rare phenomenon.

Collaboration is most common in mature fields with development of strong paradigms (Bayer and Smart 1988). Scholarship in immature disciplines or new specialties of established fields is often characterized by theoretical articles produced by single authors. This period of "lone wolf" exploration is needed at the ground-breaking stage of a field to define its boundaries and clarify its conceptual framework (Patel 1973). Mature fields with well-defined paradigms, on the other hand, tend to move from theory building to theory testing. Once paradigms are in place, "a 'pack' of scholars at their cooperative best, operating . . . under conditions of a cumulative body of knowledge, access to specialized skills, . . . technical facilities, [and] methodological sophistication," set out to confirm or revise their field's dominant theories

(Patel 1973, p. 92). Collaboration is also more widely practiced in areas that require sophisticated instrumentation and facilities and in fields that typically receive generous financial support from outside sources. In most cases, these are the fields with the highest development of paradigms.

The so-called "hard" sciences (chemistry, physics, for example) are at the high end of the collaboration spectrum, the "soft" sciences (like sociology and political science) at the low end. Collaboration is not widespread in the humanities. It is more common in the social sciences, and it is almost the norm in the physical sciences (Finkelstein 1984).

A distinction between "word disciplines" and "data disciplines" represents another way to separate fields engaging in high collaboration and low collaboration (Berelson 1960). In data disciplines like biology and physics, single-author rates in one study were only around 30 percent, while in word disciplines like history and philosophy, single authorship accounted for 80 to 95 percent of the publications in any given field (Berelson 1960). Some fields (psychology or anthropology, for example) have subdivisions in each camp, and the amount of cooperative scholarship of these groups varies accordingly. Perhaps most interesting from the perspective of this monograph, however, is the overall trend in collaborative scholarship. Multiauthor publications (and, presumably, collaborative scholarship) in both data and word disciplines increased, compared to single-author publications, from 1949 to 1979 (Over 1982).

The distinctive nature of the various disciplines helps to account for their differing practices in collaboration. In fields with esoteric theoretical structures that require elaborate technical facilities (like physics and chemistry), it is relatively easy to specify and allocate research tasks (Fox and Faver 1984). In contrast, in fields with less theoretical justification for any particular arrangement of tasks or priority of concerns (English literature or history, for example), division of labor is not as clear cut or as plausible. Scholars in a field like physics are nearer to a consensus in matters relating to theory, methodology, and training than are sociologists or political scientists, because the physicists have more highly developed paradigms. Paradigms serve to specify what the research questions are and how they can be most productively pursued (Gibson 1987). For this reason, hard scientists report experiencing fewer disagreements with colleagues than do their colleagues in the soft fields. Academics in the natural sciences also indicate that they are more likely than professors in the humanities and social sciences to be influenced by their colleagues and are more prone to co-author publications (Finkelstein 1984).

Development of strong paradigms could promote collaboration in several ways. Virtual consensus on the major research questions and methodologies in a field imbues scholars with a sense of shared purpose that makes increases in collaboration and multiple authorship inevitable (Gibson 1987). This high degree of consensus creates a climate conducive to interaction and cooperation (Finkelstein 1984). Studies have found that researchers in the hard sciences are more socially connected with their colleagues in research than are their counterparts in the humanities and the less paradigm-driven social sciences (Biglan 1973; Lordahl and Gordon 1972). Paradigms serve to foster collaboration by making the steps in the research process more routine and less dynamic, enabling researchers to get things done by planning work in detail, by setting realistic deadlines, and by delegating many clearly defined tasks to less-skilled subordinates (Hargens 1975).

Though collaboration occurs in the humanities, it is less normal than collaboration in the sciences. The nature of the dominant form of scholarship in the humanities explains this difference. Humanities scholars work differently from other researchers in terms of the types of material required, their approach to this material, the time frame within which they operate, and their extent of immediate contact with other researchers (Stone 1982). They do much of their work independently in libraries and archives. Many humanities scholars find it extremely difficult to delegate tasks like literature searches. The subjective interaction between the humanist and his or her material is a distinctive feature of humanities scholarship (Stone 1982), inhibiting the sharing of research tasks and prolonging the time required to complete humanities scholarship. The standard belief in the humanities is that "humanistic knowledge results from the application of one mind investigating a slice of reality and interpreting it anew in the context of that individual's total experience and understanding" (Reagor and Brown 1978, cited in Stone 1982, p. 294).

It would be unfortunate, however, to overlook the collaborative activity that does occur in humanities scholarship. Most intellectuals cannot create in total solitude, and interaction with colleagues is essential to the development of ideas (Cosner 1965). Moreover, writing is a social and collaborative act that depends on an author's discourse with interpretive communities (Bruffee 1984). Examples abound of productive collaborations among authors: Joseph Conrad and Ford Maddox Ford, Thomas Wolfe and Maxwell Perkins, Samuel Clemens and Charles Dudley Warner, among others (Brady 1988).

Collaboration in the arts is more common than one might expect. The collaborative nature of art is often obscured by the myth of the hero, which gives us a van Gogh without a Gaugin or a Cezanne without a Pissarro (Shapiro 1984). The best of modern art "will be seen to partake in a conscious way in the spirit of collaboration" (Shapiro 1984, p. 46). Impressionism, cubism, surrealism, and abstract expressionism are each communal movements. Collaboration in art does not erase an individual's identity, nor does it necessarily result in shared products. "In the best collaborations, individuals maintain their own peculiar flavors and resonances but are struck by the new alliance into added forms that could never have been discovered by any of the 'players' singly" (Shapiro 1984, p. 53).

Certainly the nature and the frequency of collaboration vary across disciplines. Contrary to conventional wisdom, however, collaboration occurs in virtually all fields of study.

Variations within Fields

Not surprisingly, the amount of collaboration varies within as well as between fields. Many disciplines cover topics ranging from highly theoretical issues to complex quantitative problems. For this reason, the subdivisions of a single discipline could differ considerably in their collaborative practices. Several studies have documented this variation. In one study of the field of astronomy, for example, much higher levels of co-authorship characterized observational as opposed to theoretical work, and collaboration was especially common in rapidly growing areas of astronomy that employ sophisticated instrumentation (Gordon 1980). Within anthropology, multiauthor collaboration occurred primarily in biophysical and archaeological anthropology, very little multiauthor work in the sociocultural and linguistic subdivisions (Choi 1988). Psychology occupies a similar in-between status. Psychological journals oriented toward conceptual analysis, literature reviews, and professional activities are less likely to publish collaborative papers than are data-oriented journals (Over 1982). But psychology could gradually be moving into the data or hard science camp, becoming more data oriented and requiring the greater specialization in skills that promotes a team approach to research and increasing multiple authorship (White, Dalgleish, and Arnold 1982). Apparently the move toward greater collaboration is a selective trend, fostered by the changing circumstances of subject fields and evolving professional demands. The variation in collaborative practices across and within disciplines suggests that the move toward collaboration is not simply a universal development affecting all professors in the same way.

Costs of Collaboration in Research

Scholars who collaborate generally reap many benefits from their efforts. The investment involves costs as well as dividends, however. Three primary costs are associated with collaboration—time, financial, and socioemotional (Fox and Faver 1984).

Any successful collaboration requires an investment of time. Researchers must be willing to interact regularly to monitor the project's progress and adjust activities as necessary. Maintenance of a collaborative project consumes more time than maintenance of independent research, because decisions have to be worked out with all parties involved to be credible (Tomlinson, Semradek, and Boyd 1986). The time required to maintain a well-oiled collaboration grows as groups become more diverse. For example, when collaborators from different fields have different scientific goals and speak different scientific languages, they must invest more time to complete a mutually satisfactory project (Hagstrom 1964).

Collaboration involves significant financial costs as well. Telephone calls, postal expenses, and duplicating charges are necessary to maintain any kind of long-distance collaboration. Often collaborators find it necessary to interact face to face, which of course requires transportation that can cost a substantial amount (Fox and Faver 1984).

The socioemotional costs of collaboration probably receive the least thought when peers consider working together, yet they could actually be the most costly form of investment collaborators make. Working closely with colleagues inevitably leads independent-minded academics to differences of opinion. Stresses and strains can result as collaborators attempt to maintain good working relations while remaining true to their own professional standards and priorities (Fox and Faver 1984). The socioemotional costs of collaboration can be especially high for women and minorities. Individuals who differ from the dominant group in an organization (white males on most campuses) could have more difficulty establishing and maintaining collaborative relationships that will enhance their work performance and benefit their career advancement (see "Critical Issues Regarding Collaboration" later in this monograph).

Carried to extremes, collaboration can threaten an individual's professional identity—especially for scholars who have not gained recognition on their own. "No doubt some collaboration between a strong master and a disciple can lead to pathos, problematic identification, and desiccation" (Shapiro 1984, p. 55). The artist Michelangelo is a case in point. "Through collaboration [he] produced some elements not within his own painting vocabulary. In the process, however, the collaborators were diminished as independent beings" (p. 55). Under the current academic reward system, collaboration can prove especially costly to junior academics who do not have a solid record of independent publications to their credit (Fox and Faver 1984).

A good collaboration, somewhat like a garden, requires careful nurturing to achieve its full potential. The longer a collaboration continues, the more time is required to maintain a working partnership. The initial enthusiasm that characterizes early collaborations often wanes eventually (Wildavsky 1986). Working teams typically experience burnout after about 18 months of intense activity (Kanter 1983). Hence, occasional breaks should be built into a team's schedule to keep it energetic and creative.

Collaboration offers scholars a means of achieving goals that might otherwise be unreachable. Yet it requires sacrifices that independent researchers do not have to make. Academics who wish to collaborate successfully must be ready to invest

A good collaboration, somewhat like a garden, requires careful nurturing to achieve its full potential.

the time, money, and emotional involvement necessary to function as a unit.

Empirical Evidence of Collaboration's Impact

Very few empirical studies examine the outcomes of collaborative research compared to the results of independent scholarship and the impact of collaborative working relationships on individual or group performance (Aram and Morgan 1976). Likewise, no distinct body of research assesses the outcomes of various types of collaborative arrangements (Smart and Bayer 1986). Evidence from a variety of sources, however, suggests that the relationship between collaboration and performance is complex and not necessarily direct.

As discussed earlier, research on collaborative learning arrangements indicates that collaboration usually leads to higher performance than do independent or competitive learning situations. Indeed, group performance in solving problems is superior to the independent work of even the most expert group members (Johnson and Johnson 1983). The rationale for this differing level of performance is simple. People who work cooperatively succeed because "a group is greater than the sum of its parts" (Kohn 1986, p. 61). In contrast, noncooperative approaches to solving problems usually involve duplication of effort, which wastes both time and talent (Kohn 1986).

When the focus is more specifically on scholarly productivity, however, the evidence favoring collaborative approaches is less clear-cut. A number of researchers report that collaborative approaches are positively correlated with productivity. A study of university chemists concludes that collaborators of various types publish more than researchers who work alone, and chemists who work in pairs or in larger teams have significantly more publications than colleagues who do not collaborate (Bayer and Smart 1988). This pattern appears to be true for other fields as well. The most productive scientists tend to have a record of more co-authored publications than do less prolific colleagues in their fields (Meadows 1974); thus, this analysis of communication in science concludes that high publication productivity among individuals tends to be linked with above-average co-authoring of papers. In sum, the available empirical evidence does suggest that collaboration and scholarly productivity are positively linked. Prolific researchers in many fields collaborate more often than do their colleagues in general. Yet studies on collaboration do not clarify exactly how collaboration enhances productivity. To what extent collaboration stimulates increased productivity or to what extent it is primarily a coincidental activity of people who would be highly productive in any circumstance remains to be determined.

Collaboration's link to quality of research is an even more complex phenomenon. Some studies provide evidence that collaboration results in a better product than independent research does. Other studies, however, report inconclusive findings on the relationship between collaboration and quality of research.

Publication statistics show a positive correlation between the number of authors on a paper and the probability that it will be accepted for publication (Gordon 1980; Presser 1980). The connection between collaboration and quality might not be as direct as it initially appears, however. The distinction between single-author and multiauthor articles in one study was not in the "accept" and "reject" categories but in the "reject" and "revise and resubmit" categories; thus, collaboration might not necessarily result in very good research reports (Presser 1980). Rather, collaboration seems to help scholars avoid making mistakes or submitting bad work that the scholarly community will not accept. Furthermore, enhanced quality in collaboration could be situational rather than universal (Presser 1980). The relationship between collaboration and the acceptance rate of publications is somewhat stronger in masters-granting than in doctoral-granting departments, suggesting that collaboration is particularly helpful to academics in minor departments that might lack the number of specialists needed to conduct scholarship on the cutting edge in many fields today. Academics who have nearby colleagues and adequate support might not reap the same rate of return on an investment in collaboration.

Related evidence on quality reveals that the most prestigious journals in several fields (biology, chemistry, physics) contain a disproportionate number of collaborative papers when compared to less recognized journals in these same fields (Beaver and Rosen 1979). This finding likewise suggests that collaboration performs a function of quality control that increases the chances a co-authored paper will be published.

Findings on the impact of research publications, another measure of quality, do not offer such strong support for the

merits of collaborative research and writing. A study of multi-author publications in sociology found that single-author articles (54 percent) were slightly less likely than multiauthor articles (62 percent) to be cited in subsequent published articles. Indeed, this investigation concluded that single-author publications were more apt to have a low impact on their field (one to two citations in subsequent publications), whereas multiauthor publications tended to have medium impact (three to six citations) (Oromaner 1975).

The findings of other analysts are not necessarily parallel, however. A review of 1,300 articles in seven fields revealed an inconsistent relationship between an article's impact and the number of its authors, and considerable differences were found within and between fields (Lindsey 1980). In some cases, co-authored work had more impact, in others, single-author publications. A study of three applied fields found that multiauthor articles typically yield a greater number of citations (from 18 to 64 percent more) than do single-author papers (Smart and Bayer 1986). Yet "only in Management Science did the [multiauthor] works garner a statistically significant higher citation rate than [single-author] works" (p. 301). "Sparse and insignificant evidence" (p. 303) exists to suggest that co-authored publications have more impact on their fields; overall, collaboration has little impact on "aggregate quality, regardless of field, as measured by citation indices" (p. 303).

Taking risks and enhanced creativity are other outcomes often attributed to collaborative scholarship. The assumption is that teamwork serves as a source of sustenance and support when researchers challenge the conventional wisdom of their fields and propose alternative paradigms (Fox and Faver 1984). Some evidence suggests that a positive relationship does exist between collegial cooperation and risk taking. For instance, the "highest levels of communication and organization are achieved by groups in the process of formulating a radical conceptual reorganization within their field" (Griffith and Mullins 1972, p. 960). Collaborative processes in corporations serve to reduce risk, guarding against failure and encouraging completion of projects. Research that specifically examines the relationship between collaboration and risk taking by academic scholars is very sparse, however. The same is true for research focusing on collaboration and creativity. Evidence exists that productive controversy resulting from the group's debates and the exchange of diverse views fosters originality of expression and creative problem solving (Johnson and Johnson 1987). Other studies do not offer such vigorous support for the creative benefits of collaboration, however (see, e.g., Aram and Morgan 1976). Researchers in one study concluded that their study did not invalidate assumptions about collaboration's connection with creativity and problem solving, but the authors did not provide documentation confirming that teamwork is strongly related to risky, innovative research (Aram and Morgan 1976).

Personal and professional benefits to individuals are another argument sometimes advanced in support of more collaboration. Members of effective work teams in corporations tend to express very high levels of satisfaction (Lawler 1986). Teams that operate well fulfill human needs for social interaction and belonging, forces that are, at best, ignored by independent scholarship. Successful teams also respond to competence, achievement, and recognition (Lawler 1986). Collaboration promotes psychological well-being by avoiding the processes of coercion and compromise that characterize more hierarchical working arrangements (Aram, Morgan, and Esbeck 1971). The study of a research and development team found a significant association between collaboration and the opportunity to meet team members' needs for self-actualization (Aram, Morgan, and Esbeck 1971). Admittedly, relevant data are limited, but they do suggest that collaboration can enhance the quality of academic work life and bolster faculty morale.

Research on the outcomes of collaboration demonstrates that joint scholarship often leads to positive results. But the evidence is not as consistently supportive as advocates of collaboration with colleagues might wish. Perhaps most surprising is the limited amount of empirical study of collaborative arrangements and their overall results. Clearly, more research is needed to clarify under what conditions collaboration yields sufficient benefits to make joint endeavors with colleagues cost-effective in terms of both economic and human resources.

When Collaboration in Research Is Not Appropriate
This section documents the complexities inherent in collaborative working relationships. Many factors must be synchronized for collaboration to succeed, and many variables

can lead well-meaning colleagues to fail in their attempts to work together. It should be obvious from this analysis that collaboration is not always the best research strategy for academics to employ. A team approach is appropriate:

> . . . for purposes closely related to staying ahead of change: to gain new sources of expertise and experience; to get collaboration that multiplies a person's effort by providing assistance, backup, or stimulation of better performance; to allow all of those who feel they know something about the subject to get involved; to build consensus on a controversial issue; . . . to build commitment; to tackle a problem [that] no one "owns" by virtue of organizational assignment; to allow more wide-ranging or creative discussions/ solutions than are available by normal means . . . (Kanter 1983, pp. 242–43).

In contrast, collaboration is not appropriate when one person has far more expertise on a subject than all of his or her potential partners, when little time is available for people to work together, or when individuals work more effectively alone (Kanter 1983). Perhaps the ultimate key to successful collaboration is interdependence. To work well together, the group must be engaged in tasks that have certain interdependent elements (Lawler 1986). If nothing can be gained by looking at the problem from different perspectives or delegating aspects of the work to persons with special skills, collaboration can waste valuable time. Only when collaborators believe they can produce something together they cannot accomplish alone is it wise to enter the complex realm of cooperative research and writing.

COLLABORATION IN TEACHING

The teaching arena of professional work provides another vehicle for faculty collaboration. Most of the literature concerning faculty collaboration in teaching at the postsecondary level is descriptive, often consisting of the reports and reflections of faculty who have participated in such arrangements. While team teaching is used at all educational levels, the impact of team teaching has been evaluated primarily at the elementary and secondary levels. Nevertheless, the descriptive literature, coupled with some evaluative reports on specific courses and programs, is useful for developing a basic picture of the types of collaborative teaching college and university faculty engage in and for identifying the advantages, limitations, and problems associated with this form of collaboration.

Forms of Collaboration in Teaching

Team teaching is a prominent form of faculty collaboration. The following definition of team teaching applies across all educational levels and is sufficiently broad to encompass the range of team teaching models:

> *The team system is an organizational device by which a number of persons work together in a concerted effort to perform related instructional activities and to achieve common educational goals* (LaFauci and Richter 1970, p. 1).

Categorizing the models of team teaching is difficult because those who have written about it use diverse terms and emphasize different variables (see, e.g., Daniels 1984; Flanagan and Ralston 1983; LaFauci and Richter 1970; Polos 1965; Rinn and Weir 1984; Tims 1988). Three dimensions, however, stand out as useful in categorizing forms of collaborative teaching: (1) the roles faculty participants take and the relationships of faculty team members to each other; (2) whether the collaboration is interdisciplinary, multidisciplinary, or within a single discipline; and (3) whether the collaboration involves one course or a set of interrelated though independent courses (cluster courses). In addition to these three dimensions, team teaching arrangements vary in terms of the number of faculty members involved. The literature provides examples of teams ranging from two to five or more members.

The following subsections discuss various forms of team teaching, organizing them along the three dimensions just

---

mentioned: varying faculty roles, interdisciplinary versus multidisciplinary approaches, and cluster courses. A fourth subsection discusses a form of collaboration in teaching that differs significantly from team teaching. The buddy system or, as it has been dubbed through the late Joseph Katz's work with New Jersey colleges and universities, the Master Faculty Program offers a vehicle through which faculty members can provide feedback to each other and discuss their teaching, though they are not engaged in the co-teaching implied by team teaching.

Models focused on faculty roles and relationships
The roles faculty members assume in collaborative teaching arrangements and the ways in which they relate to each other as team members can take a variety of forms. In particular, formats for team teaching vary with regard to the degree of hierarchy versus equality among the faculty members and the degree of interaction among the team members. In some models, one faculty member takes the lead while the other team members take less time-consuming and less involved roles. In some models, all faculty team members are present throughout class meetings while in others the faculty members each teach for only part of the course. If a team is teaching several sections of a course, each professor might teach all the sections for a specific period (perhaps a month) after which another faculty member takes over, or each professor might teach his or her specialty to each section, with the team members rotating across sections.

Five types of collaborative teaching arrangements have been described, each differing in the nature of roles the faculty colleagues assume (Easterby-Smith and Olve 1984). In a "star team," one teacher takes the responsibility for the class and is the primary professor, but he or she invites experts to meet with the class as particular topics are addressed (also termed the "master-teacher pattern" [Polos 1965]). For example, in an introductory psychology class, one professor would meet regularly with the class but would invite other colleagues each to visit a class session to discuss their particular specialties, such as child development, group processes, clinical issues, or sports psychology.

A "hierarchical team" is one in which a more senior faculty member plans the course and offers regular lectures, while more junior faculty or teaching assistants lead regular discussion groups with sections of students. This model is perhaps the most familiar to both faculty and students, as large undergraduate courses in many fields are taught in this format. Like the star team, this model involves differing levels of responsibility and a hierarchical relationship among the team members.

In the other three models, team members bear equal responsibility for the course. Faculty members of a "specialist team" bear joint responsibility for design of the course but divide teaching duties according to individual expertise. If the team is teaching multiple sections of a course, faculty members using the specialist model rotate among the sections to enable each professor to teach his or her specialty. One example of this model is an optometry class taught by three instructors who jointly developed the philosophy, goals, and plan for the course and then divided the responsibilities for teaching according to expertise. One team member coordinated scheduling, equipment, and administrative details, and all team members were expected to attend the classes frequently, provide feedback to their colleagues concerning teaching plans and style, and participate in evaluating students (Heath, Carlson, and Kurtz 1987).

A fourth model is the "generalist team," in which course planning and responsibility are shared as they are in a specialist team but teaching responsibilities are not necessarily divided among members on the basis of special expertise. Team members might simply divide their individual time in class according to their schedules or other factors. For example, they might alternate teaching every few days or every few weeks.

The fifth model in this categorization, the "interactive team," differs from the previous four in that team members both share all responsibility for the class (a nonhierarchical collaboration) and are present together in all classes. Team members collaborate in all aspects of planning the course, preparing exams, and grading, and they meet regularly to discuss the course, the students, and their teaching. Some interactive teams, especially when just two faculty members make up the team, literally co-teach by jointly discussing with each other and the students the day's topic. Other interactive teams use an "observer-participant" format, in which one lectures and the other serves as a discussant and observer (Flanagan and Ralston 1983, p. 116). The roles of lecturer and discussant-observer alternate each class session. In this form of interactive teaching, also called "intracoordinated team teaching" (Flanagan and Ralston 1983), the observer interrupts the lecturer to ask questions, clarify points, and develop other perspectives. Additionally, the team members meet after class so the observer can help assess students' learning and attitudes and can offer suggestions regarding teaching style to the lead teacher. Students reportedly react positively to the variety involved in this team teaching model (Flanagan and Ralston 1983).

Examples of the interactive team illustrate the interesting pairing that can occur. In one instance, a physicist and speech therapist teamed to teach a speech science course that showed students the contributions made by physics to speech therapy (Duckworth and Lowe 1986). In teaching health education to medical students, community physicians and health education officials have worked closely together (Tannahill and Robertson 1986). In another example, a faculty member in industrial marketing was teamed with a librarian. Because students needed to use the library for some of their assignments, the team of two collaborated to develop and refine the assignments and to teach the course. They held workshops in the library during which the instructor explained what kind of information was necessary to do the work and the librarian showed which sources would be useful and how to find them (Tims 1988).

Models that vary by disciplinary integration
Some observers of team teaching categorize the models not according to faculty members' roles but according to disciplinary integration (Daniels 1984; Rinn and Weir 1984). An interdisciplinary model of team teaching "is planned and taught as if knowledge were one and the disciplines had not yet been invented" (Rinn and Weir 1984, p. 5). Typically, interdisciplinary courses draw on materials from various disciplines to explore and analyze a particular theme or issue (such as, for example, women's studies, environmental issues, or community in American society). The emphasis, however, is not on the distinct disciplines, but on what light the disciplines in concert can shed on the topic or issue. Faculty teams usually involve two to four faculty members, with different disciplinary homes, who meet frequently and teach

together in the kind of integrated format described in the interactive team model (Rinn and Weir 1984).

Multidisciplinary courses also focus on broad themes and topics but preserve disciplinary distinctions as the topic is studied. Team members are drawn from different disciplines, and each discusses the topic with the class from his or her particular disciplinary perspective. The focus is on the different emphases and concerns of the various disciplines in dealing with the topic. Faculty participants involved in multidisciplinary team teaching typically work less closely together than those participating in the interdisciplinary approach (Rinn and Weir 1984). Their roles are likely to be most characterized by the specialist team model.

Faculty collaboration might be neither interdisciplinary nor multidisciplinary. Each of these approaches to collaboration implies the collaboration of faculty from different disciplines. In contrast, two or more faculty members within a single discipline or department can collaborate to teach a course, each bringing his or her specific areas of expertise to the course.

An interdisciplinary model of team teaching "is planned and taught as if knowledge were one and the disciplines had not yet been invented."

The cluster course model
While the term "team teaching" usually implies two or more faculty working together to teach one course, it also can refer to faculty efforts to coordinate separate courses in different disciplines. The faculty who teach such clusters of courses are engaged in a coordinative team teaching model (Rinn and Weir 1984). The courses arranged in a cluster each relate to a broad topic and develop different aspects of the topic. For example, a biology course and a geology course might each concern ecological issues, with students taking the two courses concurrently or sequentially (Rinn and Weir 1984). The courses each have a departmental home, and each is taught by a different faculty member. The extent of faculty interaction in the cluster course model can vary from periodic meetings to inform each other what the other is discussing to more regular meetings to modify the courses so that common themes can be developed in a complementary way. At the University of Hartford, where this model is implemented in the form of an integrated cluster of independent courses, one-hour weekly seminars taught jointly by the various faculty in the cluster serve to integrate ideas and themes that span the particular courses (Daniels 1984). When faculty involved

with cluster courses work closely together to plan and link their courses, they move toward the multidisciplinary model.

The buddy system (the Master Faculty Program)

Faculty members can engage in ongoing collaboration around their teaching without involvement in team teaching. Another form of collaboration is the pairing of faculty for regular interaction regarding their teaching and their students' learning. The state of New Jersey has taken the leadership in developing and encouraging this form of collaboration among the faculty of its colleges and universities. Originally under the guidance of the late Joseph Katz and now sponsored by the New Jersey Institute for Collegiate Teaching and Learning, the Master Faculty Program has spread to include many faculty on a number of campuses. The philosophy undergirding the program is that faculty members can collaborate to understand better how students learn and how their teaching affects students' learning.

The Master Faculty Program is essentially a "buddy system" in which faculty work in teams of two. One faculty member serves as a regular observer in a colleague's course, visiting once a week for the course of the term. While in the class, the observer pays particular attention to the teacher's style, the pacing of the class, the reactions of the students, and issues of interest to the two collaborators. Each team could choose to focus on different elements of the teaching/learning process. Both faculty members each regularly interview several students to discuss the students' thoughts about the course, their learning process, their preparation for class, their concerns, and any other issues that arise. In addition to the regular observations of the class and the interviews with the students, a third component of this model of collaboration consists of regular conversations between the two faculty members. The team members might be observers in each other's classes during one term, or they might work together over two terms, reversing roles after a semester. Once a month, all the teams on campus convene to discuss their experiences and ideas (Katz and Henry 1988; Rice and Cheldelin 1989).

Evaluation of this program (Rice and Cheldelin 1989) indicates it has a strong impact on participants. Team members report their appreciation of the opportunity to explore teaching issues in depth with a colleague, acknowledging that such interchange of ideas regarding teaching and students' learning does not occur often in higher education. They also report new insights into how their students learn and the implications for their approaches to teaching. Of interest also is that the students interviewed often show enthusiasm for the opportunity to provide their feedback as well as to interact regularly in conversation with a faculty member.

The Master Faculty Program currently is being adapted and implemented at a number of colleges and universities throughout the country, and other buddy arrangements are used on some campuses. Some attempts at faculty development, for example, pair a junior faculty member with a senior professor to ensure that mentoring occurs. The two colleagues observe each other's classes, exchange feedback, and share ideas about teaching methods, classroom style, subject matter, and students' learning processes (see Austin 1990 and Boice 1990, 1992 for ideas about variations on mentoring pairs).

Outcomes of Faculty Collaboration around Teaching
While an extensive literature systematically evaluating and assessing the outcomes of faculty collaboration in teaching does not exist, the various articles and reports describing approaches and examples of team teaching taken together provide some evidence of the strengths and drawbacks of team teaching. Additionally, ongoing monitoring of New Jersey's Master Faculty Program has been under way for several years. The report of this monitoring (Rice and Cheldelin 1989) corroborates a number of the advantages of faculty collaboration in teaching that are mentioned in other descriptive articles.

Strengths and advantages
When faculty collaborate around their teaching, three kinds of benefits occur: development of their teaching ability, new intellectual stimulation, and a closer connection to the university or college as a community.

First, with regard to the development of teaching ability, collaboration through team teaching or buddy arrangements provides a vehicle through which the participants can discuss ideas, hopes, and concerns about their teaching and their students (Ware, Gardner, and Murphy 1978). The culture in most universities and in some smaller colleges typically does not encourage faculty members to find regular time to reflect on and exchange ideas about their teaching. As colleagues collaborate over time, the trust can be developed that is necessary if substantive and open conversation is to occur. Collaboration also enables faculty members to get new ideas about their teaching styles and their other classes as they observe the methods, style, and approaches colleagues use (Fuchs and Moore 1988; Rinn and Weir 1984). The revitalization can be one of the most powerful effects of the collaborative process for participating faculty:

> *Since the Greeks, dialogue has been acknowledged as one of the finest methods of learning. While teaching, the instructors are drawing from each other and from themselves both factual and conceptual knowledge that might otherwise lie dormant. Lecturing in isolation, individual instructors lack both the insightful criticism and exposure to alternate styles necessary to expand, rethink, and reform presentations, thus denying to themselves the accessibility of ongoing renewal* (Quinn and Kanter 1984, p. 1).

The revitalization takes place not only through observation of one's colleagues. Team teaching and faculty pairing to visit each other's classes also involve peer evaluation (Heath, Carlson, and Kurtz 1987). Feedback and constructive suggestions from peers can provide the information and impetus for faculty members to try to improve their teaching. And through collaborative teaching, the potential exists for faculty members to get to know their students more closely (LaFauci and Richter 1970). If faculty team members discuss students' progress and learning during team meetings, they can become more responsive and observant regarding the students' reactions. As described, the Master Faculty Program emphasizes this attentiveness to students' learning as a primary function of the faculty team. (It should be noted that if a faculty team is teaching a very large class, as sometimes occurs with team teaching, the number of students could mitigate the opportunity for closer faculty-student interaction.)

A second benefit for faculty that can result from collaborative teaching is the opportunity for new intellectual stimulation. As team members discuss their respective contributions to a course and describe the particular perspective each brings, they can discover ways in which their disciplines relate as well as perspectives, ideas, and interpretations revealed

by different disciplinary perspectives. Disciplinary special-
izations can be shared and broader knowledge added for
those faculty members who collaborate in their teaching. Further, depending on the expertise of the members of the team,
collaboration can help faculty members link research with
practice—useful for both students and faculty (Fuchs and
Moore 1988). Intellectual benefits can derive from collaborative teaching arrangements:

> *Team teaching can be wonderful, as both faculty and stu-
> dents are "surprised by joy" when they make hitherto unseen
> connections and experience the lovely rigor of intellectual
> activity* (Rinn and Weir 1984, p. 10).

The third benefit for faculty members who collaborate is
a diminishing of the isolation associated with the autonomy
professors historically enjoy (Fuchs and Moore 1988). In large
universities especially, faculty members often have few occasions to connect with colleagues in other disciplines. Collaborative teaching, when faculty members from different
departments are teamed, can challenge and diminish the barriers between disciplines and, on many campuses, between
departments (LaFauci and Richter 1970; Rinn and Weir 1984).

Faculty collaboration in teaching affects not only the professors themselves, but also the students. Team teaching that
brings diverse disciplinary perspectives to the study of a topic
helps students gain "an appreciation of the essential connectedness of all knowledge" (Rinn and Weir 1984, p. 7). As
they hear more than one view, they can sort ideas, learn to
assume different perspectives, and contrast and synthesize
knowledge and ideas (Daniels 1984). Disagreements among
their teachers about a topic illustrate for the students that
interpretations vary, and faculty members' willingness to
reveal the limits of their knowledge may show students how
intellectual growth occurs. Additionally, with a team-taught
course, students have a variety of role models and are more
likely to encounter an array of pedagogical approaches to the
subject under study (Rinn and Weir 1984). As mentioned earlier, collaboration along the model of the Master Faculty Program is designed specifically to help faculty team members
become more aware and attentive to their students' learning
processes. Students cannot help but benefit from such explicit

faculty concern with their progress (Katz and Henry 1988; Rice and Cheldelin 1989).

Collaborative teaching holds implications for the curriculum as well. Team teaching, especially involving faculty from different disciplines, addresses "the hardening of curricular arteries" that departmental turf could encourage (Rinn and Weir 1984, p. 7). As faculty members team teach or observe in courses outside their specialty, they may gain an enhanced appreciation of the contributions that other disciplines and perspectives can make to the students and to their own work. This appreciation among colleagues is useful if the institution intends to undertake any curricular innovation or reform. Another way in which team teaching can affect the curriculum is by opening an avenue for the establishment of new courses that have no obvious departmental or disciplinary home. Courses in ethnic studies and women's studies have been initiated and ultimately established firmly at some institutions through this route (Rinn and Weir 1984).

Limitations and concerns regarding collaborative teaching

A realistic assessment of the pros and cons of faculty collaboration around teaching points to several potential tensions. First, collaborative work, especially in teaching, takes time. Faculty collaborators must fit team meetings into their schedules to handle the necessary planning and coordination involved in team teaching and to nurture the trusting, open relationship essential to a productive relationship. The amount of time needed for interaction varies with the kind of team teaching, but, if the course is designed on the interactive model or the interdisciplinary model, success depends on frequent and extensive meetings among the faculty colleagues (Fuchs and Moore 1988; Rinn and Weir 1984).

Faculty also might be initially uncomfortable with the loss of autonomy inherent in successful collaboration. Because teaching is typically a solitary activity, some adjustment is required to the presence of another faculty member in the classroom. Furthermore, collaborators not only must become accustomed to sharing their authority and space with colleagues, but also must find ways to blend their teaching styles in ways that foster students' optimal learning (Fuchs and Moore 1988; LaFauci and Richter 1970).

Two other challenges may arise when faculty members collaborate in their teaching. Professors whose responsibilities for team teaching involve teaching their specialties to different sections of a large class could be plagued with boredom from repeated presentations (Ware, Gardner, and Murphy 1978). In contrast, those collaborators who interact to teach a course whose topic extends beyond each faculty member's specialty could find that the broadening of focus required to participate fully conflicts with disciplinary pressures to publish in and stay abreast of their specialization (LaFauci and Richter 1970).

Finally, while team-taught courses offer students variety, diverse perspectives on a topic, and the opportunity to learn from a number of professors, they also have the potential to fall short of these advantages. If faculty members do not take the time to coordinate and plan as a team, the quality of class sessions can be disjointed, unorganized, repetitive, and un-even (Heath, Carlson, and Kurtz 1987; Rinn and Weir 1984). Faculty collaborators must be aware of these potential problems to ensure the likelihood of a productive course and successful collaboration.

Collaborative teaching, like collaborative research, fits within the expanded conception of academic scholarship (Boyer 1990). Teaching that encourages professors to learn from one another and to adopt interactive modes of instruction promotes greater intellectual community and hence vitality among faculty. Although collaborative teaching presents professors with some difficult challenges, it offers a flexible mechanism for enriching academic careers and for responding to the complex instructional tasks professors confront as the new century approaches.

THEORY, STRUCTURE, AND PROCESS OF COLLABORATION

Collaborative endeavors can begin through formal arrangements or through more informal interactions that develop into joint work; in either case, however, the success of the collaboration requires the participants to give some attention to issues of process. The following reflections on collaboration in multiparty community and business issues pertain equally to academic collaboration:

> The importance of process cannot be overemphasized in planning and conducting successful collaborations. Good-faith efforts to undertake collaboration are often derailed because the parties are not skilled in the process and because insufficient attention is given to designing and managing a constructive process. Good intentions are insufficient to counteract the typical dysfunctional dynamics that interfere with productive group performance in work groups . . . (Gray 1989, p. 93).

This section addresses the issues of process—the "how"—in collaboration. The discussion focuses first on the theoretical dimensions of collaborative processes, offering a theory of collaboration, outlining critical dynamics of collaboration, identifying the theorists of group process whose work helps those seeking to understand collaboration, and providing several theoretical models for analyzing and understanding the process and work of collaborative teams. Second, the section takes a more practical, applied perspective, discussing important roles and characteristics of effective team members as well as the characteristics of effective teams, and outlining the specific steps typically involved in successful faculty collaboration.

Theoretical Dimensions of Collaboration

While various organizational and group theories elucidate aspects of academic collaboration (and are discussed later), the single theory that is most useful for analyzing and understanding these team efforts among faculty is the theory of negotiated order, which conceptualizes collaboration as "a mechanism by which a new negotiated order emerges among a set of stake holders" (Gray 1989, p. 227). Among negotiated order theorists (Day and Day 1977; Goffman 1983; Strauss et al. 1963; Strauss 1978), "negotiated order refers to a social context in which relationships are negotiated and renegotiated. The social order is shaped through the self-conscious interactions of participants" (Gray 1989, p. 227).

The development of "joint appreciation" (Trist 1983, cited in Gray 1989, p. 229), through which the collaborators share their perceptions of the issue or problem and make agreements about the dimensions of their work together, creates the negotiated order. "Essentially, these agreements constitute a normative framework through which members correlate their activities with respect to the problem. In so doing, they establish a temporary order for the domain" (Gray 1989, p. 229). As they work together, collaborators each contribute and identify their own interests and then, trying to involve as many interests as feasible, reframe the problem and search for approaches. The negotiated order emerges through the team's search for a jointly agreed-upon perspective and approach (or approaches) (Gray 1989, p. 239).

Negotiated order theory emphasizes not only the dynamic, process-oriented elements of collaboration, but also the "temporary and emergent character" of this form of work (Gray 1989, p. 233). According to the theory, collaboration is a vehicle through which individuals with related interests connect with each other. As "negotiated orders," however, the connections could take a variety of forms; they could be short and temporary, develop into long-term normative agreements, or become permanent institutional arrangements (Gray 1989, p. 235).

Describing collaboration as a form of negotiated order emphasizes five critical dynamics of successful processes (Gray 1989). These dimensions also seem applicable to collaboration among faculty members. First, collaboration involves interdependence among the participants. Individuals are motivated to collaborate to work toward goals that are not possible or feasible for one person alone to achieve. Second, through collaboration, partners encounter new views and approaches, and, by grappling with the differences between their views, participants find new understanding, ideas, or solutions. Third, joint ownership of decisions is necessary for successful collaboration; that is, collaborators must all agree on the direction of the joint work. The fourth key dynamic is closely related to the third. If collaborative relationships are to be productive, participants (or "stake holders") must share responsibility for decisions about the team members' relationships and roles. Finally, negotiated order theory emphasizes that "collaboration is an emergent process" (Gray 1989, p. 11) through which the roles of participants, their decision-making processes, and their goals and agreements evolve over time. While this application of negotiated order theory to understanding collaboration is particularly informed by analysis of the joint work of community agencies, a focus on action research teams similarly emphasizes the dynamic and emergent quality of collaboration:

> As a team moves forward on its project, research tasks change, demanding different forms of interaction, different roles, and different patterns of behavior. As team members work through interpersonal issues, their understanding and perceptions of the project change, they interact differently, and they approach their research in new ways. How a group interacts over time thus influences the development of their research project, the project's outcomes, and the quality of the experience for group members (Oja and Smulyan 1989, p. 55).

While negotiated order theory is particularly useful as a way to understand collaboration, other research and development of theories in the behavioral sciences also provide a base of knowledge about group process. The earlier research has contributed to understanding about teams, explaining that these contributions have dealt both with the internal dynamics of groups and issues of leadership (Parker 1990). A pioneer in the study of group dynamics studied how groups behave and the reasons for their actions (Lewin 1951). Particularly useful for examining a group's functioning has been Lewin's force field analysis, with its attention to the team as an open system and the forces that affect the functioning and work of the team. *The Human Side of Enterprise* (McGregor 1960) focuses on a theory of motivation within groups and on the characteristics of effective and ineffective teams. Another theorist whose work on groups has been seminal found that more effective managers are "employee centered" and those least effective "job centered" (Likert 1961). Another study of management style linked with a team's effectiveness developed a managerial grid and posited that the most effective leaders exhibit strength on two key dimensions, concern for production and concern for people (Blake and Mouton 1964). This body of work in organizational and group theory provides

Individuals are motivated to collaborate to work toward goals that are not possible or feasible for one person alone to achieve.

the social science framework within which a conceptual view of collaboration among faculty can be placed. A particular strand of research in group dynamics focuses on the phases or stages through which teams move, the focus of the remainder of this subsection.

The theories and research on small-group interaction and team development all emphasize that a team—or collaborative group—is constantly changing and evolving. Conclusions about stages of development are a dominant theme throughout much of the theoretical work on small groups and teams:

> *Research in group dynamics suggests that members of a group work through sequential or cyclical phases of group development and establish and maintain group norms, decision-making processes, patterns of communication, roles, and interpersonal structures. The group's negotiation of these aspects of its interaction affects its goals and results* (Oja and Smulyan 1989, p. 55).

The following brief summary of several theories of group development offers a variety of windows for understanding the process of collaboration among faculty. While each theory is distinctive, they share an emphasis on the dual challenges that confront collaborative groups, however; that is, both interpersonal and task issues must be handled if collaboration is to be successful and productive.

Group interaction is a cyclical process, somewhat akin to changing a tire, where the bolts are tightened in sequence and then the sequence is repeated (Schutz 1958, cited in Oja and Smulyan 1989). This theory posits three phases: the "inclusion phase," the "control phase," and the "affection phase." During inclusion, members often discuss small issues or their biographies as a route to become acquainted. Critical issues to be handled at this phase are interpersonal boundaries and members' commitment to the group. In the control phase, members deal with the issues of sharing responsibility and distributing power and control. Elements of this task-oriented phase are establishing rules and procedures, structuring decision making, discussing the group's orientation to its work, and dealing with competition and struggles for leadership. The emphasis of the affection phase is on the group's socioemotional issues and needs and how they relate to the decisions made about the group's structure, decision-making processes, and tasks. During this phase, group members might express hostility, jealousy, or positive feelings toward each other. As these issues are resolved, the group cycles back to the concerns of the first phase.

Others conceptualize just two stages of group development, emphasizing the interpersonal issues confronting groups (Bennis and Shepard 1956, cited in Oja and Smulyan 1989). In the first phase, labeled "dependence," members deal with the leader's authority, perhaps coping with dependence on the leader by discussing issues external to the group's work and sometimes revolting against the leader. During the second phase, "interdependence," group members grapple with conflicts around identity and intimacy and perhaps form subgroups. By passing through these two phases, a group becomes mature, capable of resolving internal tensions, and able to act as a team.

Another theory explicitly addresses both the interpersonal and task issues confronting groups (Schein 1969, cited in Oja and Smulyan 1989). In the first of two phases, a group must handle issues of power, influence, and control, and members must establish goals, roles, and levels of intimacy about which all can agree. During this phase, members might challenge each other, withdraw, or look for alliances, but, with time, they move beyond the interpersonal to the task issues. The second phase of the group's development is characterized by attention to such task functions as gathering data, clarifying issues, and establishing consensus and to such maintenance functions as compromising and encouraging.

Another three-phase model purportedly applies to any form of collaboration (Gray 1989). The first phase, called "problem setting," involves defining the problem to be addressed and identifying the "stake holders," or interested parties. If stake holders are to be active collaborators, they each must feel committed to the collaboration and must feel they are respected by the others as team members. Attention also must be directed to the way in which responsibility will be divided, the identification of a convener skillful in group work, and the identification and securing of any necessary resources. During the second phase, "direction setting," stake holders "achieve coorientation" (p. 75), a sense of how each collaborator considers the issues and their importance. This phase involves laying out ground rules for interaction, setting an agenda, organizing subgroups to work on the task, exploring options for the group's work, and establishing agreement among participants. During the third phase, "implementation," collaborators make sure their agreements are carried out and modify their plans as necessary.

While these theories are useful in simplifying group processes by delineating two or three stages—and thereby focusing attention on critical dimensions of the life of a group—a more recent theoretical model emphasizes the complexities and nuances of group process (Srivastva, Obert, and Neilson 1977):

> *Srivastva, Obert, and Neilson (1977) recognize the complexity of group development by suggesting that a group grows along six dimensions: members' relations to one another; members' relations to authority; the group's relation to its organizational environment; the group's task orientation; the group's orientation to learning; and the group's mode of reacting to its larger environment. In each of these dimensions, the group moves through five stages, shifting from individualistic and dependent modes of interacting, through stages of competition and conflict, to a stage of cooperative independence [that] allows for task concentration and performance (Obert 1983). This perspective on group development reflects both the interpersonal and task demands a group experiences as well as the group's changing interaction with the environment within which it works* (Oja and Smulyan 1989, p. 58).

Of the various theories that have been advanced to explain how teams form and work, the one that seems most widely cited (Tuckman 1965; see also Tuckman and Jensen 1977) identifies several stages through which a successful team passes, though it acknowledges that a collaborative group can become stuck, making it ineffective. The stages are forming, storming, norming, performing, and adjourning. During the forming stage, a testing time, group members become acquainted, orienting themselves to the task and deciding how they will do the work. During storming, team members might conflict with each other, express hostility toward or frustration with the group leader, resist the task, and develop polarized subgroups. Though conflictual, this stage is very important for the group's development to avoid later resistance or diminished creativity. When the norming stage is reached, the team overcomes the interpersonal conflict and resistance to the task and moves toward trust, openness, sharing of ideas, and the ability to handle disagreement without personal anger. The performing phase involves a focus on accomplishing the task. The team has structure and can function, periodically assessing itself and celebrating successes. Finally, during adjourning, team members face issues of separation and the conclusion of their work.

This model, which can be used to analyze the development of any team, seems to be one of the most useful theoretical models for understanding the stages through which faculty collaborators pass. Each model discussed, however, can be used as a lens through which to examine and understand faculty collaboration. All the theories and models emphasize both the interpersonal and task issues that confront collaborative groups. Without attention to each of these domains, a team of collaborators will have difficulty being productive and successful and feeling personal satisfaction with the experience.

Practical Dimensions of Collaboration among Faculty

While the theoretical models suggest useful ways to understand the collaborative process, those interested in engaging in collaboration or encouraging colleagues to do so will want to consider the practical details of successful team work. Three important areas to review are characteristics of effective team members, factors associated with effective collaborative teams, and the steps involved in establishing a collaborative faculty team.

Characteristics of effective team members

Individuals who are effective as collaborative partners typically have command of an array of important interpersonal skills. They are good communicators, able to listen and to speak and write clearly. They can negotiate and have some ability in resolving conflicts. They have skills in facilitating and enabling and exude a sense of respect for the knowledge, abilities, and skills contributed by other team members (Geyman and Deyrup 1984).

Team members often take on different roles so that the group as an entity functions efficiently and effectively. Effective team members do not all function and participate in the same ways. Some members might keep their roles all during the collaborative process, while others might vary their roles, depending on what issues the group is handling (Oja and Smulyan 1989). A simple categorization of roles collaborators can assume divides tasks from maintenance. Partners who define their roles in terms of tasks encourage the group to focus on its goals, provide necessary information, emphasize the clarification of issues, and urge the group to evaluate its process and accomplishments. Collaborators more oriented toward maintenance encourage positive interpersonal relations among team members, assist in working through disagreements, and foster the interdependence of the team's members (Oja and Smulyan 1989).

Teams need members with diverse skills and orientations, for those with differing styles can be helpful at different times in the group's process (Parker 1990). Four different styles for the team's members are possible: the contributor, the collaborator, the communicator, and the challenger. Contributors are task-oriented, complete their tasks efficiently, and urge the team toward its goals. Dependable partners, they are eager to share any information or knowledge they have with the other team members. Collaborators, like contributors, also are highly committed to the team's goals but are distinguished by their willingness to forgo individual recognition in favor of the team's success. They are helpful in taking on extra work, if necessary, in addition to their own assignments and in striving to find and develop consensus among the team's members. Communicators, oriented especially to the process aspects of the collaboration, are particularly valuable as facilitators who help with the team's formation, exhibit strong skills in listening and communication, and provide encouragement and feedback to the group. Communicators assist the group in handling and maintaining the critical interpersonal dimensions of its work. And challengers serve the group by acting as a kind of prod. They are the team members who ask difficult questions, challenge the goals and leadership of the group, and urge that reasonable risks be taken. Their commitment to the team's success leads them to be very frank and honest and to hold the group to the highest standards (Parker 1990).

Various team members' skills become particularly useful at different times during collaboration. Using the phase model discussed earlier (Tuckman 1965), one sees that collaborators could be especially important in the forming stage by helping

to provide structure so the group can establish its purpose. Communicators, with their ability to listen and assist others to share views and disagreements, play a critical role during storming. During norming, contributors can urge the development of norms of excellent work, and during performing, the prodding and questions of the challengers are a guard against the team's complacency or stagnation (Parker 1990).

Particularly important is the role of team leaders in collaboration. Sometimes team members share leadership, each taking on a more prominent role at certain times, depending on his or her interests and abilities. In other situations, one faculty member becomes the primary author or lead teacher, thus holding a more permanent leadership role. In either case, those assuming leadership in a collaborative group need the ability to muster enthusiasm, hold up a vision of the group's goals, resolve conflict and build consensus, and manage both the short-term and long-term work of the team (Parker 1990). Good leaders model good collaboration.

Finally, faculty members who wish to be successful at collaboration must be able to recognize when they are becoming ineffective team members. Sometimes those involved in collaboration carry their style too far (as a task-oriented person or a process-oriented person or, more specifically, as a contributor, collaborator, communicator, or challenger), which could hinder the balance of styles necessary for a successful team. Partners might become impatient or intolerant of other team members as the work intensifies or deadlines approach (Parker 1990). Collaborative partners also become less effective if they fail to meet their obligations or neglect the guidelines established by the group. Partners in collaboration must recognize the critical role that each member plays if the joint effort is to succeed.

Factors associated with effective collaboration

Just as some of the characteristics of effective team members can be identified, so also can some factors associated with effective collaborative groups. The many forms of collaboration that characterize academic research, however, make it impossible to define a simple formula that will guarantee successful collaboration. The literature on collaboration is mostly atheoretical, and little empirical evidence currently exists on what makes faculty teams effective. What is clear is that numerous factors influence the operation of collaborative teams and, hence, their overall performance (Cohen, Kruse, and Anbar 1982). There are "no rules or formulas for making participation work that substitute for sensitive judgment of leaders about how to make trade-offs in a particular situation" (Kanter 1983, p. 276). Because of the number of factors that interact in a collaborative setting, a contingency approach is needed to understand what variables contribute to successful collaboration under what circumstances (Nobel 1986).

The team's composition. Several factors are sufficiently critical to the operation of any collaborative effort that they deserve close examination. For example, the composition of a research partnership or team greatly affects its operation and accomplishments. The proper composition of a research team depends on the task at hand. The types of collaborators needed to conduct research in nuclear physics are different from those needed to do survey research on sociological subgroups. Groups achieve maximum productivity when they contain as many members as are needed to perform the tasks and supply the interaction skills necessary to complete their assignment (Seaman 1981). The correct mix of skills is essential (Kanter 1983). The best team is comprised of individuals who are "somewhat different in attitudes, backgrounds, and experiences but not radically different" (Seaman 1981, p. 45). Other researchers concur (see, e.g., Marquis 1963, cited in Smith 1971; Pelz and Andrews 1966). Their research suggests that scientific consultation among colleagues is most productive when those involved are neither very similar nor very different. While, for example, a dissimilarity of ideas and intellectual approaches could result in constructive stimulation, major personal differences could lead to destructive conflict (Smith 1971). The middle-of-the-road approach is desirable in most collaborative settings (Fox and Faver 1982). The most productive collaborative associations are based on similarity in some areas and complementarity in others.

Several factors must be considered when attempting to assemble a workable collaborative team, including the values and goals of collaborating partners, their work habits and standards, the nature of the task to be completed, and the size of the group. Most authorities on collaboration (for example, Brady 1988; Eaton 1951; Seaman 1981; Tomlinson, Semradek, and Boyd 1986) agree that shared values and common goals are essential prerequisites to successful cooperative re-search—which does not mean that collaborators must have uniform professional beliefs or agree on every aspect of a joint project. What is highly desirable, however, is that cooperating scholars possess shared values relative to the purpose of their collaborative effort (Parker 1990; Tomlinson, Semradek, and Boyd 1986). They need to have common goals for their project. Mutual objectives provide collaborators with a clear direction and criteria for evaluating their success or failure (Seaman 1981). Potential collaborators should make explicit the values and attitudes relevant to a proposed project so that the group can assess its compatibility (Tomlinson, Semradek, and Boyd 1986). The bottom line is clear: Without shared goals and a strong commitment to the collaborative process, successful collaboration is not viable (Brady 1988; Parker 1990; Tomlinson, Semradek, and Boyd 1986).

Collaborators' respective orientation to work is another factor that has important implications for the success of their cooperative activities. Although effective collaborators might differ on intellectual factors, they probably need to match rather than complement each other on their basic approach to work. Scholars who maintain drastically different work habits will probably have difficulty forming a workable partnership (Fox and Faver 1982). Among the factors that could derail a partnership are the collaborators' work pace, energy levels, attention to detail, and concern with organization and order in work (Fox and Faver 1982). Differing standards of quality can also be a source of friction. Any of these factors can hamper a team's progress if they make it difficult for individuals to work together.

The team's size. The group's size is another key variable related to the overall performance of collaborative arrangements. No optimum or even maximum size can easily be prescribed. Research on group dynamics indicates that on a given task, a group's performance seems to decline as the group increases in size. On the other hand, larger groups perform better on some kinds of tasks because they contain larger numbers of knowledgeable and able people (Zander 1979).

Much of the literature on collaboration cautions against large teams, however. In general, as groups grow larger, the number of problems they experience also increases proportionately. Communication becomes more complex and indirect, as large groups find it difficult to interact directly on a regular basis (Seaman 1981). The potential for disagreement on substantive and methodological issues grows as more people are involved in a research project. Typically, more time is required for meetings and telephone conversations to negotiate plans and delegate responsibility (Fox and Faver 1982). As a team expands, each individual's share of the burden and sense of responsibility for the group's performance could diminish. Personal gratification from a job well done could decrease as well (Seaman 1981; Zander 1979). In sum, as groups increase in size, creative energies could be diverted from primary goals to logistical arrangements required to keep the team functioning smoothly.

The team's structure. The team's structure is also a factor that influences how collaborating groups operate. "Equality of power and authority is not unconditionally the best structure" for collaborative arrangements (Nobel 1986, p. 4). Indeed, no single type of structure is always superior. A team with a certain social structure will perform better for a particular task than teams with other structures (Nobel 1986).

Although no consensus emerges from the literature on the best structural arrangements, agreement is widespread that some clear and consistent structure is preferable to no structure at all. The absence of structure, formal or informal, in a research team inhibits the interaction and communication essential to collaboration (Fennell and Sandefur 1983).

Elaborate rules and rigid bureaucratic structures are not necessary to ensure successful collaboration, but smooth functioning requires a clear idea of authority and operational procedures. Clear structural arrangements enable group members to work within established boundaries in an autonomous, creative, and efficient way (Fennell and Sandefur 1983; Kanter 1983). If a team's operational structure is not sufficiently clear, the team could flounder unproductively, because it is difficult for its members to function cooperatively as a unit.

Communication. Communication is closely intertwined with the group's structure. Hence, it is another key feature associated with the success of collaborative activities. For example, research documents that the amount and pattern of interaction within research and development teams influences the performance of this type of collaborative unit (Nobel 1986). A great deal of dialogue is required for collaboration to work in most cases. Communication enables team members to work out common goals, resolve differences, and strengthen each individual's commitment to a joint project. Often considerable negotiation, discussion, and compromise are needed to initiate and move a project forward. In effective collaborative groups, members encourage the expression of diverse views, because they know that such exchange enhances the quality of the team's work. Similarly, effective collaborators understand that civilized and respectful disagreement is normal and useful as a group of people work together. Thus, effective teams learn how to handle conflict productively. A group cannot progress if the partners in a project do not exchange ideas and come to some meeting of minds regarding goals for the project and individual responsibilities. Ultimately, effective collaborative groups achieve consensus, a point at which each member feels he or she has been heard and everyone then agrees to support the decision of the majority (Brady 1988; Parker 1990).

Related to the communication that enhances the success of collaborative work is the extent to which an informal climate pervades a group's interactions. In effective teams, members are comfortable with each other, and humor and relaxed conversation are elements of group meetings. Team members are active listeners, providing verbal or nonverbal responses to those speaking. Each member knows that his or her contribution is important and valued (Parker 1990).

The structure of collaborative teams helps to shape the process of communicating. When the structure of a team is ambiguous, members might find it difficult to communicate efficiently. The more explicit the formal structure of interdisciplinary research teams, the more likely it is that team members will engage in the level of communication necessary to maintain an interactive joint effort (Fennell and Sandefur 1983). Structure becomes increasingly important to communication as teams of collaborators become larger and more diverse. Problems in communication are intensified when people from various disciplines try to work together. Colleagues from differing fields do not necessarily share professional conventions that ease communication. Professional norms, vocabulary, and standards that facilitate collaboration within a particular subject area can become stumbling blocks

In effective collaborative groups, members encourage the expression of diverse views, because they know that such exchange enhances the quality of the team's work.

to cooperation across disciplines. The unequal status of team members from various fields can also lead to problems in communication (Fennell and Sandefur 1983). For this reason, a well-defined structure that specifies channels of communication and levels of authority might be required to facilitate some forms of collaboration.

The most effective communication structure for a research team is determined by situational phenomena, including the type of task to be completed. Centralized communication with a clear leader/authority figure is usually best when the task is relatively simple and straightforward. In contrast, decentralized communication with many overlapping channels is often more effective for jobs that are ambiguous and complex and require creative solutions (Nobel 1986).

Differences in status. The status or prestige of cooperating scholars influences the role they play in research partnerships. The nature of their communication, the force of their ideas, and their level of influence within a team are all related to their perceived professional status. To some extent, well-defined differences in status can facilitate collaboration by automatically imposing an inherent authority and decision-making structure (Fox and Faver 1982). Research on small groups demonstrates that individuals assembled to work as a team organize themselves along lines of status or prestige even when no formal group structure is provided (Fennell and Sandefur 1983). When differences in team members' status are ambiguous, however, team members could find it difficult to work together. "Expectations of appropriate deference and dominance . . . will not be commonly shared" (Fennell and Sandefur 1983, p. 198). As a result, disagreements over goals and strategies could prove difficult to resolve, and tensions could develop from bruised egos. The motivation to communicate and cooperate can be diminished by such social strains (Fennell and Sandefur 1983).

A hierarchy based solely on distinctions in status, on the other hand, can be counterproductive as well. Hierarchical teamwork violates a fundamental assumption of professional ethics—the belief that each qualified individual is a creative source of knowledge and should be treated as an equal partner (Eaton 1951). The contention that a hierarchy of power not based on real differences of skill and contributions to a cooperative project can be counterproductive to scholarly creativity still rings true 40 years later.

As mentioned, it would be naive to assume that collaborators always function best as a democratic community of peers. "Because a peer alliance lacks an authority structure, more time and energy must be invested in decision making and problem solving" (Fox and Faver 1982, p. 333). Some research-related decisions are made better unilaterally than in consultation. Collaborators must differentiate between important decisions requiring dialogue and those that can be delegated to save time for the creative aspects of the joint activity (Eaton 1951).

The theory of status concordance postulates that research teams operate most effectively when they are organized and function in a manner consistent with the external status of the various team members. For example, when senior researchers from highly prestigious disciplines have more influence in the group's decisions about research than junior researchers from less prestigious disciplines, they are operating as a concordant team. Research on interdisciplinary collaborative groups, however, suggests that status within research teams is a more dynamic phenomenon than the theory suggests. Status concordance "facilitated effective coordination only during the early phases of team development" (Gillespie and Birnbaum 1980, p. 49). Initially, a high level of status concordance enabled new teams to define tasks, distribute resources, and organize communications. As time went on, however, external status played a decreasingly significant role in the coordination of the teams studied. Once a team is established, factors more directly related to its operation become a more salient basis for a team's status system. Variables like relevant expertise, time to devote to the project, and access to needed resources eventually supersede external status criteria (Gillespie and Birnbaum 1980). In other words, as a team develops its own identity, its method of assigning status becomes more closely related to the team's successful operation.

The group's cohesiveness. The group's cohesiveness is another factor that influences collaborators' performance. Cohesiveness is "an affective force maintaining group membership based on the rewards of social interaction" (Dailey 1978, p. 1580). Cohesive groups give high levels of emotional support to their members. Cohesiveness tends to be greater in groups that share values and are relatively small. Single-sex groups tend to be more cohesive than mixed-gender groups (Zander 1979). Typically, cohesiveness increases with a group's age. After four or five years of working together, however, the cohesiveness of many groups begins to diminish (Pelz and Andrews 1966). Cohesiveness could decrease because long-established groups know each other so well that they no longer feel a need to communicate regularly.

Research examining several attributes of teams found that cohesiveness was positively related to collaborative problem solving and the team's productivity. Evidence also suggests that cohesive teams are more innovative than less cohesive research teams (Farris 1973, cited in Dailey 1978). In fact, cohesiveness was a stronger predictor of collaborative problem solving than was the team's size, task interdependence, or task certainty.

The relationship between cohesiveness and successful collaboration is complex, however. The team's cohesiveness does not guarantee productive collaboration. Other characteristics of the team and the task affect the outcomes of teamwork as well. It is possible for a team to be highly collaborative and productive without being cohesive (Dailey 1978). For example, specialists in subject matter who divide a research problem into discrete elements might collaborate effectively yet be very individualistic in their work patterns. Likewise, a team can be highly cohesive but not very productive. Indeed, a cohesive team could actually outlive its creative usefulness but seek to stay together to maintain its socioemotional benefits (Dailey 1978).

Essentially, cohesiveness is a desirable element but an insufficient ingredient in a recipe for successful collaboration. Other conditions must be present in the proper mix for collaborative efforts to achieve their goals. To determine the role of a team's cohesiveness in successful collaboration, a contingency approach is recommended that acknowledges the interactive relationship of the team's and the task's characteristics (Dailey 1978).

The group's age. The length of time collaborators work together is another factor that influences the performance of a research partnership. Based on data from 83 groups, in general the scientific contributions of groups gradually decline as groups age, with a curvilinear relationship existing between the group's age and its usefulness (Pelz and Andrews 1966). Groups seem to reach maximum usefulness at four to five years of age, and then their value begins to taper off. Several reasons could account for these findings. Older groups tend to be more relaxed, less communicative, and less competitive than younger groups (Pelz and Andrews 1966). Over time, group members also develop more specialized interests, finding their own niche within a team. As a result, a team becomes less cohesive and potentially less satisfying and productive. These observations suggest that research collaborations should not last indefinitely. Teams should continue only as long as they remain productive. Research evidence does not suggest an absolute upper limit on collaborative arrangements, however. Older groups can remain vital if they maintain the vigorous interaction and intellectual tension that characterize new research partnerships (Pelz and Andrews 1966).

Self-assessment of the group. In effective collaborations, attention is directed to both the process of the work and the intended product. From time to time, effective teams engage in self-assessment to evaluate their progress and process. Collaborators should be alert to indications that their team is not functioning effectively (some of the problems that can arise are discussed in the next section). If difficulties occur, team members would be wise to take the time to assess the details of the dilemma and consider possible solutions.

Steps in faculty collaboration
Those wishing to develop collaborative relationships should also be interested in the specific steps necessary to embark on a collaborative project. This subsection deals with such practical issues, discussing the choice of colleagues, the determination of tasks, the establishment of working guidelines, and the termination of collaborative relationships.

Choice of colleagues. Faculty members who wish to collaborate must first consider the choice of colleagues with whom they will work. If partners are not compatible on several variables, the collaborative effort is likely to be seriously undermined. Intellectual, personal, and structural factors should be considered in the choice of a collaborative partner (Fox and Faver 1982). Collaborators should strive for similarity on some dimensions and complementarity on others.

In terms of intellectual factors, collaborators sometimes try to find partners who share their theoretical perspectives but might try to team with a colleague who brings a different but complementary viewpoint or a different area of substantive knowledge. Among the personal factors potential partners should consider about each other are their perceptions of the priority to be given to the joint work, which works best if it is at similar levels, and the extent of time each has available and is free from other commitments. If partners intend to work closely, they will be most successful if they are similar in their pace of work; this factor is not as important in a long-distance collaboration, though vacation schedules could be. Additionally, energy level and work habits, including orientation to detail, organization, and order, should be similar if possible. Collaborators are also more likely to be successful if they are similar with regard to tolerance of risk, anxiety levels, and orientation toward achievement. If one partner is strongly oriented toward completing the project and the other primarily enjoys the process with much less concern about the product, difficulties are likely to ensue. The structural factors that should be considered are the ranks of the potential collaborators, their gender, and the number of collaborators to be included. Collaborations involving individuals of different academic ranks or different genders can certainly succeed but hold inherent tensions. The size of a collaborative group affects the time involved, the way in which tasks are handled, and the potential for conflict.

Division of labor. The second step in collaboration is the determination of tasks. After deciding on the project they will undertake jointly, faculty teams tend to divide their labor in one of several ways (Fox and Faver 1982; Isenberg, Jalongo, and Bromley 1987). They might share the project entirely, working together to do the research and writing. Some collaborative research teams might choose to divide the labor, with each working on the same section and then combining their individual work into one piece. Another variation is to divide the project so that each collaborator is solely responsible for specific parts. A study of collaboration in scholarly writing found that 38.4 percent of the faculty collaborators studied worked totally as a team, meeting to talk and develop their ideas and then revising and editing each other's sections. Another 34.1 percent took a different approach, in which a primary author developed a first draft, a secondary author critiqued it, and the primary author revised it. The mode of work reported by a small group of collaborators (12.6 percent) was for individual authors each to develop separate sections of a co-authored outline or presentation (Isenberg, Jalongo, and Bromley 1987).

Decisions about how to divide the work should depend on the nature of the tasks, the skills and interests of the partners, the time and resources available, and the extent to which each collaborator wants control over the whole project. Generally, collaborators jointly engage in brainstorming and planning, while they divide the more routine responsibilities, such as verifying references (Fox and Faver 1982).

Establishing work guidelines. A third step in the process is to discuss and agree on the guidelines for the collaborative work (Fox and Faver 1982). Partners must establish a timeline and develop a schedule. A particularly important issue is the consideration of authorship and order of names on any manuscripts produced. Additionally, collaborators must attend to such issues as open communication, trust, and honesty. Failure to set guidelines can result in some of the stumbling blocks discussed in the next section.

Terminating a collaboration. Finally, a collaborative team must identify and clarify the end of the collaboration. If team members have developed friendships through the process of collaborating, the conclusion of the joint work could raise issues of separation, as often occurs when small groups conclude their interaction. In some cases, faculty collaborators might decide that their joint work was sufficiently successful and satisfying so as to lead to further work together. In such a case, the partners should be careful not to assume that their earlier successful experience precludes the need to pay explicit attention to questions regarding division of labor and guidelines for the next joint endeavor.

—o—

It should be apparent from this section that no simple model of an idealized collaborative arrangement would be of any value. So many variables interact in the operation of a research partnership that each new collaboration is distinctive in many ways. This fact should not obscure the common attributes that characterize most research collaborations. The size and composition of research teams and their operational structure and patterns of communication are some of the key variables that relate to the effective performance of collaborators, and each factor deserves careful consideration as two or more scholars pool their resources to reach a goal none of them could achieve as effectively on their own.

CRITICAL ISSUES REGARDING COLLABORATION

Along with the benefits associated with faculty collaboration come a host of complex and controversial by-products. Awarding proper credit for authorship is a thorny issue that seems to defy a standard solution. Evaluating individual contributions to collaborative teaching and scholarship is a second type of difficult issue that results when colleagues work together on common goals. Ethical questions of exploitation and abuse of subordinates or colleagues of lower status are problems that too frequently emerge in collaborative arrangements. Faculty and administrators in higher education must be cognizant of the sensitive issues collaboration often raises. Only in this way can they work to prevent problems that can derail collaborative efforts before they bear fruit.

Recognition of Authorship
Whenever academics collaborate, the potential arises for ambiguity about the relative importance of each person's contribution to the eventual product of the joint endeavor (Over 1982). Several particularly difficult questions surround collaborative authorship. Collaboration raises questions about who is and who is not an author on a research paper (Holmes 1989). What distinguishes a major contribution worthy of authorship from a minor contribution that does not deserve credit for authorship? (Bridgwater, Bornstein, and Walkenbach 1980). What are an author's rights and responsibilities in a collaborative arrangement? At what stage in the process should authorship be discussed? What is the protocol for settling disagreements that sometimes arise over credit for authorship? (Holmes 1989).

Even when collaborators agree on who the authors of a particular publication should be, conflict concerning the order of authorship can erupt. The fundamental question is "What distinguishes a 'major' contribution from the 'principal' contribution (deserving senior authorship)?" (Bridgwater, Bornstein, and Walkenbach 1980). In a meritocracy like higher education, it is not sufficient to recognize all contributors to a joint publication. The system demands to know who contributed more and who contributed less to the collaborative endeavor.

Over time, informal conventions have developed in an attempt to resolve some of the most common questions concerning authorship. Some academic disciplines list all authors in alphabetical order, regardless of their effort in producing a publication (Meadows 1974). Other fields insist that credit for authorship reflect the significance of an individual's contribution to a book or article. Occasionally, scholars agree to credit authorship on the basis of the collaborators' seniority. What is most obvious at present, however, is the lack of consistency across higher education and even within many fields of study. No standardized policies enable collaborators throughout academe to prevent disputes about authorship. Nor do any universal policies or practices permit deans or department heads to assess the magnitude of an individual professor's contribution to a jointly produced publication.

"The scientific norm of universalism prescribes recognition be accorded to the producer of knowledge solely on the merit of one's product, regardless of extraneous factors such as academic status or gender" (Heffner 1979, p. 377). Indeed, this norm is widely applied in many branches of science. Authors are typically listed in the order of the importance of their contribution to the reported research, with the principal contributor coming first (Meadows 1974). Some fields, such as psychology, have explicitly legislated policy consistent with the norm of universalism. According to Principle 7f of the American Psychological Association's "Ethical Standards of Psychologists":

Publication credit is assigned to those who have contributed to a publication in proportion to their professional contributions. Major contributions of a professional character made by several persons to a common project are recognized by joint authorship, with the individual who made the principal contribution listed first (American Psychological Association 1983, p. 20).

Some strongly favor this approach to authorship, believing the strategy of listing authors sequentially in accord with their relative contributions permits the scientific accountability and reward system to function effectively within the collaborative arrangements that characterize much of contemporary scholarship (Over 1982).

The criterion of universalism often is not used, however, in distributing credit for authorship, for it is frequently easier in some fields than in others to set criteria for judging the importance of collaborators' contributions (Over and Smallman 1973). It is sometimes difficult to identify those truly responsible for a particular piece of work (Heffner 1979); hence, it is problematic to reward individual contributors appropriately. Likewise, it is nearly impossible to assess relative contributions in collaborative work (Lindsey 1980, p. 150).

The difficulty of assessing contributions to authorship probably accounts for the widespread use of other schemes for ordering authors' names on joint publications. When it is virtually impossible to distinguish among the contributions of various authors, it is customary in many fields to cite authors alphabetically (Meadows 1974; see also Zuckerman 1968). This trend is especially common when the number of authors exceeds two. A similar pattern even occurs when only two authors are involved (Lindsey 1980). Overall, "in a collaborative team the member whose name occurs first alphabetically is more likely to appear first in a list of authors" (p. 149).

Recognition of authorship is sometimes determined by less straightforward criteria. For example, the function of a publication should be considered when the sequence of authors is determined (Weinberg 1989). If the objective of the publication is to attract funding for research or to secure tenure or promotion for a faculty member, it might be desirable to base order of authorship on those considerations.

Occasionally, decisions about authorship are based principally on seniority, with senior scholars listed as the only authors or the principal authors of a publication. In this situation, people with less experience or lower status receive less credit than their veteran colleagues, regardless of the merits of their individual contributions. Likewise, nominal authorship, when individuals like laboratory directors or faculty advisers are listed as authors even though they did little to produce a specific publication, awards credit for reasons at best tangential to the preparation of a book or article. Generally, the literature that addresses the issue of credit for authorship discourages practices of this sort. In principle, credit for authorship should not be awarded, even to people of higher status or authority, unless they have contributed substantively to the project reported on in a publication (Shawchuck, Fatis, and Breitenstein 1986; Spiegel and Keith-Spiegel 1970). In practice, the academic community frequently fails to adhere to this policy.

Until consistent practices for attributing authorship are established, confusion over who deserves credit for what scholarly contribution is likely to persist. In the meantime, some believe that distributing credit for authorship equally is the best course (Narin 1976). According to this scheme, each author receives the same fraction of credit for a jointly produced work. While this recommendation has surface appeal as a simple solution to a very complex scholarly problem, it is unlikely to win many supporters under the current system of academic evaluation and reward that encourages competition and distributes resources and recognition on the basis of individual, not collective, productivity.

Determining authorship on criteria that have little to do with the actual contributions that made a publication possible poses a serious problem for higher education. When it is not possible to judge who is truly responsible for a scholarly work, quality control is difficult to maintain. When accountability is attenuated, factual errors can go undetected, and the source of ethical violations cannot necessarily be identified. For this reason, as collaborative scholarship becomes more widespread, fair and consistent guidelines for recognizing individual contributions to jointly produced publications are sorely needed throughout the academic community.

Criteria for awarding authorship

Although no general consensus exists within the academic community on how to distribute credit for authorship fairly, relevant research findings on this topic provide collaborators with a basis for decision making when confronted with difficult questions of authorship. Two studies of psychologists indicate a fair amount of agreement within that field on what activities deserve recognition for authorship (Bridgwater, Bornstein, and Walkenbach 1981; Spiegel and Keith-Spiegel 1970). While two researchers found diverse opinions about how specific types of contributions to research should be recognized, they did uncover a generally held opinion that designing a research project and writing the final report for publication more clearly deserved senior authorship than did conducting the experiment and analyzing the data (Spiegel and Keith-Spiegel 1970).

A later study, although troubled by a low response rate (27.5 percent), was able to discriminate more precisely among scholarly activities deserving recognition for authorship (Bridgwater, Bornstein, and Walkenbach 1980). This study revealed substantial opinion that "research design and report writing are at the apex of the pyramid in terms of recognition deserved" (1981, p. 525). Respondents considered research design most worthy of senior authorship, with writing of the final report second. When design was an individual's only contribution to a collaborative project, respondents concluded that authorship was deserved, and they believed in some cases even senior authorship would be appropriate. In contrast, data analysis was deemed worthy of authorship only when the individual directed the analysis and wrote portions of the results section of the publication in question. Respondents to this study essentially viewed data collection and tabulation as minor contributions not deserving full authorship. The survey suggested numerous functions are worthy of a footnote rather than full credit for authorship, including providing an idea for research without being involved in the project itself, supervising data analysis, and collecting data by testing, interviewing, searching archives, or reviewing literature.

Scholarly importance of a contribution should be the principal criterion on which decisions about authorship are based. The amount of time or effort a person invests in the production of a publication is not as significant in making such decisions as is the importance of an individual's work to the overall project. Designing the research and writing up results require higher levels of knowledge and understanding of the entire project than do other, more specialized activities (Bridgwater, Bornstein, and Walkenbach 1981). For this reason, research design and report writing deserve higher recognition.

No doubt many scholars would take exception to some of the criteria emerging from two studies limited to the field of psychology. The studies' general conclusions, however, provide a foundation for judging what level of recognition is warranted by various types of contributions to a jointly produced publication. Perhaps answering a question is the best way to reach agreement about authorship: "Would completion of the project, or the paper, have been possible without the individual's contribution?" (Weinberg 1989, p. 103). If the answer is "no," the individual deserves recognition for authorship.

Scholarly importance of a contribution should be the principal criterion on which decisions about authorship are based.

Addressing problems with authorship

Ideally, questions concerning authorship should be addressed early in a collaborative relationship rather than near the end. During the initial planning of a joint project, individuals wishing to work together should delineate each partner's responsibilities and agree on the status of authorship for each contributor (Shawchuck, Fatis, and Breitenstein 1986). Often roles in a collaborative relationship evolve over time. Consequently, decisions made early in a team's life might have to be revisited and perhaps revised. To prevent misunderstandings and potential conflicts, though, it is essential to discuss authorship before collaboration proceeds too far. Team members should attempt to reach early agreement on a variety of concerns:

1. The specific responsibilities and expectations for each party;
2. Acceptable forms of acknowledgment;
3. Authorship and the order of authorship;
4. Access to the research data collected;
5. Appropriate use of the data; and
6. Expectations regarding future writing projects (O'Rourke 1989, p. 102).

Failure to resolve questions of authorship satisfactorily can lead to tension—even hostility—in a collaborative relationship. At worst, disagreements over authorship can abort the publication of a jointly written manuscript (O'Rourke 1989).

It is best to refer conflicts of this sort to a neutral third party before they evolve into a permanent impasse. An unbiased professional acting as an arbitrator can examine controversial issues from a more objective perspective than can the emotionally involved collaborators. Involving an objective individual in negotiation can help to resolve difficult issues of authorship and keep a collaborative project on track.

Evaluating Individual Contributions to Collaborations
Evaluating individual contributions to collaborative products is closely related to the issue of authorship. Questions of authorship, however, are essentially the team's problem that ideally should be worked out among the collaborators themselves. In contrast, the evaluation of individual contributions to collaborations, both in teaching and in research, often becomes an institutional problem that confronts colleagues who serve on faculty personnel committees, department chairs, deans, and other administrators with difficult questions.

Evaluating the contributions individuals make to collaborative partnerships is perhaps one of the most challenging problems collaboration presents higher education (Bayer and Smart 1988). At the same time, it is also one of the most urgent. In a competitive enterprise like higher education, individuals will probably be willing to work together over the long run only if they are adequately recognized and rewarded for their personal contributions (Eaton 1951). Likewise, quality control by the scholarly community requires that contributors to research and publication be held accountable for their work.

As the number of authors on a jointly written publication becomes larger, however, it becomes increasingly difficult to determine who is really responsible for the article's content and the background research it is based on. The "practice of multiple authorship weakens the social control [traditionally] exercised by the scientific community through the award of recognition for published contributions" (Hagstrom 1965, p. 140). Similarly, nominal authorship—the practice in which individuals who have had very little to do with a publication are listed as authors—also weakens the academic profession's ability to hold authors accountable for their work. Essentially, without careful assessment and attribution of credit for contributions to collaborative products, fraud, distortion, and other forms of dishonest or incompetent practice are difficult to identify and correct.

The issue of evaluating individual contributions also arises in team teaching. In some forms of team teaching, where faculty members each take responsibility for a section of a larger class or teach particular units, evaluating the work of each faculty member is easier. If a team of faculty share all aspects of course planning and participate in the classroom together, however, evaluation of each collaborator's individual contribution becomes much more problematic.

Given the importance of evaluation in maintaining accountability for professional work, it is surprising how little the topic of evaluating collaborative products is addressed in the literature on collaboration. This lack of information could reflect a widespread assumption that it is nearly impossible to assess relative contributions to collaborative work (Lindsey 1980). Forty years ago, the lack of adequate measures of collaborative products was noted, acknowledging the "temptation" to measure creative work with objective criteria, such as number of hours worked, number of pages written, or number of contacts made during field work (Eaton 1951). Fortunately, this strategy for "evaluation" has not taken hold. Unfortunately, no more satisfactory procedure for evaluating individual contributions to cooperative projects has won widespread support within the academic community. Weighting schemes are one option for assessing responsibility and credit for collaborative products (Lindsey 1980). For example, two-thirds of the credit for authorship could be awarded to a publication's first author, one-third to the second author, and so on. Arbitrary schemes of this sort violate the intuitive judgment of many scholars, however (Lindsey 1980). Certainly many of the contributions that individuals make in collaborative work—either in teaching or in research—are too interactive and dependent on the support of other team members to weight them so simplistically.

The bottom line is that the evaluation of individual contributions to collaborative products is virtually ignored in most reports on collaboration. Even policies for awarding credit for authorship leave many questions unanswered about how to rank the contributions individuals make to joint scholarly endeavors. These policies leave the final decisions on credit for authorship to the contributors to work out. When complex and sensitive questions of this sort must be resolved, ideally they should be answered by the parties most closely involved. On the other hand, deans, department heads, and faculty personnel committees must also make judgments about individual contributions to jointly produced documents or team teaching. They could benefit from guidelines offering fair and systematic methods to assess collaboratively produced works. Evaluating jointly produced scholarship or collaborative instruction will never be easy. No simple policy will ever take the place of thorough examination and discriminating professional judgment. Yet as collaboration becomes a more common practice among faculty, it becomes increasingly important that satisfactory strategies be developed for evaluating collaborative outcomes.

Women as Collaborators
Because white males dominate most academic fields, collaboration by individuals outside the mainstream of higher education (women and minorities) also deserves careful attention. Regrettably, few researchers have examined the experiences with collaboration of academic women. The avail-

able evidence suggests that women's collegial relationships vary from those of men, and their approach to collaboration probably differs as well (Cameron and Blackburn 1981). Women academics have a tendency toward more personalized interaction with colleagues (Simeone 1987). While men often interact with colleagues primarily on a professional basis, women tend to view their associates as colleague-friends. This pattern is evident even among highly research-oriented women professors.

The explanation for these differences could relate to the orientation to relationship and community that tends to characterize many women. *Women's Ways of Knowing* (Belenky et al. 1986) describes the themes of connectedness and human relations that frame the ways in which women construct their work, their lives, and their understandings of the world. The developmental process for women moves toward "connected knowing," whereby relationships are based on trust, empathy, mutual support, and a desire to understand the ideas and experiences of others. Given the orientation of many women toward "connectedness" rather than "separateness" from others (separateness is more likely to characterize the way in which men construct their sense of self), it is not surprising that women and men approach collaborative teaching and research relationships differently.

Perhaps individuals who represent a small minority in an organization (women in the academic profession, for example) are highly visible and are often singled out as tokens (Kanter 1977). Tokens are frequently "quarantined" or isolated by members of the dominant group. They are often excluded from certain social or business occasions, and some topics are not discussed in their presence. Based on research in corporations, "many of the women did not tend to be included in the networks by which informal socialization occurs and politics behind the formal system were exposed" (Kanter 1977, p. 227).

Similarly, research documents the difficulties women have in establishing professional relationships in the academic profession (Hood 1985; Wong and Sanders 1983). Women and minorities have a harder time establishing contacts with colleague-friends and collaborators (Hood 1985). A study at the University of California in Santa Barbara shows that this problem goes back at least as far as graduate school, where women students have trouble getting involved in master-apprentice relationships that often prove pivotal to future career development. Women graduate students are more likely than men to be excluded from protege relationships with senior faculty (Simeone 1987). The Santa Barbara study found that men tended to have advantages in gaining access to distinguished mentors. Men students were also more likely to receive research assistantships, generally regarded as more instrumental in integrating students into ongoing departmental activities and contributing to long-term scholarly performance (Wong and Sanders 1983), rather than fellowships.

Although relevant empirical data are sparse, some evidence exists that women's collegial relationships vary by academic field. For example, in physics and chemistry, equivalent percentages of men and women graduate students reported they were apprenticed to faculty members. In contrast, differences in apprenticeships between the sexes appeared in the biological sciences and mathematics (Zuckerman and Cole 1975).

Women's ties with colleagues continue to be disadvantaged following entrance to an academic career. A survey of 1,000 faculty women revealed that a feeling of isolation and the desire for networks and support groups was the second highest concern of the women sampled (Spencer and Bradford 1982). Women professors suffer from the stigma of deviancy and hence are often excluded from old boy networks that can lead to career benefits (Kaufman 1978; see also Kanter 1977). For example, male assistant professors were more likely than female assistant professors to have colleagues of higher status in their professional networks (Kaufman 1978). In contrast, female academics were more likely than males to include colleagues in their networks who have research interests different from their own. Given their differing composition, the men's networks are more likely to promote career growth and achievement than are the women's networks. And the initial exclusion of women from career networks could result in permanent exclusion from influential male-dominated networks (Kaufman 1978).

Male academics characteristically have a larger number of professional associations than do females (Cameron and Blackburn 1981). In contrast, women have larger networks of colleagues than do men (Hood 1985; Kaufman 1978). The critical distinction between men and women, however, could be in the quality rather than the quantity of their professional connections. More women than men faculty collaborate

(Cameron and Blackburn 1981), yet women are more likely than men to continue in a single collaborating relationship, whereas men tend to have multiple collaboration partners. Their differing approaches to colleagueship seem to give men a greater advantage professionally. Perhaps a large number of associations rather than a small number of intimately known colleagues serves to generate more ideas and leads to a higher rate of productivity (Granovetter 1973).

The stigma of deviancy appears to be especially pronounced for unmarried women professors. Unmarried women academics seem to occupy an even more disadvantaged position than their married women colleagues. The former are more likely to be excluded from male networks (and probably collaborative arrangements) than are married women professors (Kaufman 1978). Likewise, they have fewer males in their professional networks than do married men or women. Perhaps most revealing of unmarried female academics' deviant status is the finding that the number of men in their networks decreases with time. In contrast, the number of men in the networks of married women professors increases over time. The bottom line could be that cross-sex relationships among colleagues are "more permissible for women with the protective status of marriage" (Kaufman 1978, p. 16).

Evidence from available research provides at best an unclear picture of the collaborative authorship experiences of women. Various studies have produced inconsistent or even contradictory findings. One study, for example, found that women are just as likely as men to publish collaboratively and that women are as likely as men to be the first authors on publications (Cole and Zuckerman 1984). Other studies show that women are underrepresented as first authors of jointly authored publications. Evidence from psychology (Teghtsoonian 1974) and sociology (Wilkie and Allen 1975) demonstrates that when men and women co-author articles, women are more likely than men to be listed as second authors (see also Heffner 1979). Female Ph.D.s in one study were at least twice as likely as any other group in the sample to believe they were excluded from recognition for co-authorship that they deserved (Heffner 1979). The perception that women have been excluded from co-authorship was highest among female natural scientists. While the conclusion is not definitive that sex discrimination in awarding collaborative authorship exists because the number of female Ph.D.s in the sample was small, the literature contains considerable support for the hypothesis of sex discrimination.

The inconsistent findings suggest that many questions remain about the status of women in collaborative authorship arrangements. At present, it is impossible to say whether the differences in men's and women's patterns of authorship represent differences between the roles men and women play when collaborating or differences in the criteria by which they are allocated credit (Over 1982).

Relatively few studies compare the collaboration of men and women academics, but the available information suggests that the two genders have stylistic differences that not only influence their approach to collaboration but also their overall professional performance.

Collaboration by Minorities

Even less empirical research examines the collaboration practices of minority faculty. The research findings concerning the work-related experiences of African-American faculty, however—one group of minority faculty—suggest both that collaboration might be less frequent among African-American faculty than among their white colleagues and that it is precisely the kind of activity that could help these faculty handle difficult challenges in their work. While the number of minority students is increasing considerably, the number of minority faculty is not keeping pace. Between 1977 and 1983, the number of full-time African-American faculty dropped from 19,674 to 18,827 (American Council on Education 1988). Furthermore, the number of African-American individuals receiving doctorates fell from 1,056 in 1979 to 820 in 1986, a 22 percent decline (American Council on Education 1988). Attrition from the faculty ranks also is more likely to occur among women and minority members than among their white colleagues, leading to significant concern about "the revolving door syndrome" for these faculty members (O'Brien 1990).

High on a compilation of the difficulties facing minority scholars is the lack of professorial support from colleagues and the sense of isolation and alienation they experience (Frierson 1990; Garza 1988). The research on African-American faculty emphasizes that these academics experience isolation from their white colleagues socially, psychologically, and professionally (Finkelstein 1984; Frierson 1990; Moore and Wagstaff 1974). African-American faculty frequently have difficulties establishing the kind of networks that lead to collaboration in writing and grantsmanship, positions of responsibility in professional and scholarly associations, editorships, and consultancies. In addition to isolation and exclusion, minority faculty typically face particularly heavy expectations for their involvement in committees and departmental work, as role models for minority students, and as spokespeople for minority issues (Frierson 1990). African-American women faculty find these demands especially excessive (Peterson 1990).

While the difficulty in establishing collaborative relationships is a key feature of the minority faculty experience, recommendations to enhance the work experiences of minority faculty stress the importance and value of collaboration. For example, after careful analysis of the challenges threatening the level of African-American participation in the faculty ranks, one researcher urges African-American faculty to establish collaborations with others who share common interests and specifically with other African-American academics (Frierson 1990).

Research that examines the experiences of those minority faculty who do collaborate will further understanding in important ways both of the collaborative process and the integration of minorities into higher education. This gap in the literature on collaboration needs to be filled.

African-American faculty frequently have difficulties establishing the kind of networks that lead to collaboration in writing and grantsmanship.

Collaboration with Professional Subordinates

The role of subordinates in collaborative relationships is another critical issue that deserves the attention of higher education. Collaboration involving senior researchers and professional subordinates (laboratory technicians, research assistants, graduate students, for example) is very common in academic scholarship. Yet little research examines how supervisors treat their subordinates in collaborative situations or how subordinates are credited for their contributions to research and publications. Certainly the potential for exploitation of individuals in secondary positions exists, because senior researchers exert great influence over the lives of those they supervise. Further, senior scholars frequently are in a position to make decisions concerning the assignment of publication credit in collaborative research (Heffner 1979).

Subordinates can be exploited in numerous ways. Abuse occurs whenever assistants are used for nonprofessional (or inappropriate) work or when they are not given credit where it is due (Wildavsky 1986). Graduate students are particularly vulnerable to exploitation because their academic advancement is often subject to the approval of the same person with whom they are collaborating. "The problem with teamwork involving students arises from tension between teaching and the research assistance aspects of the relationship" (Hagstrom 1964, p. 245). Graduate students are subject to several forms of exploitation:

1. Prolongation of a student's graduate work;
2. Subordination of a student's educational interests to a professor's research interests;
3. Misappropriating credit for work a student has done (Hagstrom 1965, pp. 134–35).

The inequity in power that dominates collaborations between full-fledged scholars and subordinates presents fertile territory for abuse. Only sparse research documents the degree to which subordinates in collaborating relationships experience exploitation. While no evidence was found of a systematic withholding of co-authorship from non-Ph.D.s on research teams (Heffner 1979), some statistics do imply that exploitation is more common than it should be. It also appears to vary by field. For example, a study in 1957 found that nearly half (46 percent) of the respondents sampled agreed "major professors often exploit doctoral candidates by keeping them as research assistants too long, by subordinating their interest to departmental or the professor's interest in research programs . . . " (Berelson 1960, p. 162). Data from 12 fields seem to show that exploitation is most widespread in the laboratory sciences (Hagstrom 1965): "Major professors often exploit doctoral candidates," ranging from 57 percent in microbiology, biochemistry, and biophysics to 28 percent in the humanities, and mathematics and statistics (Hagstrom 1965, p. 134).

These statistics suggest that exploitation of subordinates in collaborative teams is a serious problem. On the other hand, the lack of recent research on this topic makes it impossible to assess the present magnitude of the problem. Higher education has a moral obligation to monitor collaborative relationships to ensure that they operate fairly and ethically. Fulfillment of this responsibility requires regular follow-up research.

In Conclusion

Most collaborators would agree that some challenging problems accompany the numerous benefits associated with collaboration. Too often higher education has ignored difficulties like the exploitation of subordinates and failure to award proper credit for contributions to jointly authored publications. The lack of good data on these critical issues could account for the failure of colleges and universities to respond systematically to these thorny problems of collaboration. The higher education community should monitor more carefully the problems associated with joint research and teaching. Likewise, higher education should develop firm policies to prevent the negative consequences that sometimes result when academics work together.

RECOMMENDATIONS FOR POLICY, PRACTICE, AND FUTURE RESEARCH

Recent reports focusing on the future of higher education (Boyer 1990; Lynton and Elman 1987) advocate an expanded and more flexible definition of the professorial role. Collaboration with colleagues is one means of enlarging academic life and making it more responsive to the evolving needs of a dynamic society. Working closely with others gives faculty, who often feel overextended, the opportunity to explore new terrain, such as the variety of scholarly modes—discovery, integration, application, and teaching—that Boyer views as major components of the professorial position. Ideally, collaboration enables professors to stay fresh and vital by adding new dimensions to their work lives.

This review of the literature on faculty collaboration shows that joint teaching and research can yield many positive outcomes—as well as some difficult problems. On balance, however, we believe that the benefits of faculty collaboration are substantial and outweigh the potential negative consequences. This section outlines a variety of actions intended to encourage more faculty collaboration and extend its benefits to a wider segment of the academic profession. We direct these recommendations at three distinct audiences: faculty members, administrators and the institutions they lead, and the higher education community in general.

Recommendations for Faculty

1. *Consider developing collaborative relationships.*

Both empirical evidence and anecdotal reports testify to the value of collaborative relationships. Faculty who collaborate tend to be more prolific and in many cases produce higher-quality scholarship than academics who conduct research and write independently. Evidence also suggests that collaborators tend to be more creative and less averse to risk than those who work alone. Personal benefits, such as greater satisfaction with work and overall psychological well-being, are correlated with collaborative activities as well. Data on the outcomes of collaboration are not universally positive. Yet sufficient information supports the benefits of collaborative relationships to recommend them as a useful vehicle for extending academic resources and enriching academic life.

We urge professors to start collaborating early in their professional lives. Studies of productive scholars reveal that they almost universally conduct research and publish early in their careers, often before completing graduate school (Finkelstein 1984). Frequently, this work is done in collaboration with a mentor or other senior academic who can introduce the junior partner to the practices and mores of their discipline and the academic profession in general. Early collaboration with positive role models can quickly orient junior academics to effective practices in teaching and research and cultivate habits needed for a dynamic and productive academic career.

We also encourage veteran academics to initiate collaborative arrangements with their junior colleagues. The benefits of collaboration are two-way. Younger academics, fresh from graduate school, can expose senior professors to recent developments in their fields, new methods of teaching and research, and fresh intellectual perspectives. Collaboration between junior and senior professors can reinvigorate the more experienced party at the same time it gets the novice partner off on the right professional track.

A professor should consider initiating a variety of collaborative relationships over the course of a career. Some active collaborators work with only one or two partners over a long time. Others have many intense but short-term collaborations. No research clearly demonstrates that one approach is superior to the other. We encourage professors to consider the merits of multiple collaborations, however, because working closely with a variety of people inevitably exposes individuals to a wider range of information and skills and more contrasting points of view than is possible from long-term collaborations with a very limited number of colleagues. Initiating new collaborative partnerships from time to time can offer the fresh insights and creative ideas that can diminish as established collaborations grow older and more predictable.

2. *Be aware of the dimensions of the collaborative process.*

Successful collaborations involve a complex set of attributes and activities, each requiring careful attention from the parties involved. Faculty who wish to collaborate should be familiar with all aspects of this process. First it is necessary to identify avenues for cultivating potential collaborative partners. Faculty should look broadly and imaginatively when seeking partners for teaching and research projects. Institutional colleagues, students, and associates one meets at professional conferences are just a few examples of a wide array of potential collaborators. Aspiring collaborators need to be familiar with the attributes of effective collaborative partnerships to organize a team that has the ingredients necessary for successful teamwork.

Potential collaborators also should be aware of the flow of the collaborative process and of the distinctive roles partners typically play. Some key issues (discussing the work pace and style of team members, establishing guidelines for the collaborative relationship, determining areas of responsibility, for example) should be addressed early in the relationship for work to progress smoothly. Similarly, those interested in collaborative relationships should develop skills in leadership, facilitation, communication, and negotiation and have an appreciation for the ways in which collaborative partners might assume different roles as they work together and as the project progresses.

Understanding collaboration also involves awareness of the potential pitfalls and problems that can emerge in any collaborative arrangement. Collaborators who understand how communication problems, differences in status, and unproductive partners can derail a team's progress can try to ward off such difficulties before they become intractable.

Above all, collaborators must learn to maximize mutual gains. Collaborative arrangements must respond to the distinctive circumstances and needs of the individual partners and ensure that each benefits from the joint effort. By pooling their intellectual resources or dividing a task too large for one person to complete in a timely fashion, collaborators can all achieve a level of quantity and quality impossible alone. But to achieve this objective, academics must learn to coordinate their efforts and forgo some of the unqualified recognition that accompanies individual achievement.

Recommendations for Administrators and Institutions

1. *Establish policies and environmental conditions supportive of collaboration.*

Colleges and universities that wish to promote collaboration should develop policies for evaluation and reward that offer incentives for collaborating. For example, institutions should encourage faculty to include collaboratively produced work in the portfolios they submit to tenure and promotion committees. To make it a meaningful exercise, institutions must design policies for adequately assessing individual contributions to collaborative projects. Too often collaborative work is discounted in the process of faculty evaluation, be-

cause faculty colleagues and administrators do not know how to assess its merits. To give sufficient credit for collaboration, departments or deans might need to set up special committees to evaluate individual contributions to team teaching or co-authored publications. Committees of this sort would engage outside experts to review collaborative work that falls beyond the domain of departmental experts (work in women's studies or American studies by a member of a history department, for example). Policies that encourage the thorough and fair assessment of collaborative work are likely to benefit the career advancement of active collaborators and indirectly encourage more collaboration by faculty in general. When active collaborators are tenured and promoted, the message goes out that collaboration is valued and rewarded.

Environmental conditions like institutional policies can either promote or inhibit faculty collaboration. Both adequate resources and time are necessary to collaborate successfully. Institutions that wish to encourage collaboration should be willing to help with the costs of travel, telephone and mail charges, and other miscellaneous expenses that collaboration often entails. Special funds providing seed grants specifically for joint projects can cover some of these costs as well as motivate independently minded faculty to work together (Office of the Assistant Provost 1990). In some cases, it might also be necessary to alter professors' work schedules or provide them with release time to enable faculty to pool their ideas and design collaborative projects.

Administrators should encourage faculty to take advantage of traditional avenues for collaboration, such as team teaching and joint research by departmental colleagues. Administrators can also foster collaboration by helping to create new avenues for collaboration outside normal structural (i.e., departmental) boundaries. Administrators have a key role to play in the establishment of study groups, centers, institutes, or other arrangements of this sort that can increase faculty interaction and prompt them to work together (Office of the Assistant Provost 1990). By providing financial and moral support for interdisciplinary team research and cross-disciplinary teaching, deans and department heads greatly expand the options for collaboration available to professors.

Institutions and their administrators can also support collaboration by recognizing it publicly. Campus newsletters and alumni magazines are ideal places to highlight the achievements of faculty partnerships and teams. Faculty meetings, receptions, and other academic and social gatherings also provide excellent opportunities to publicize the work that faculty colleagues are doing together.

2. *Engage in leadership practices that promote collaborative activity.*

Senior administrators typically are strategically well-placed to promote collaboration. They must exercise their influence carefully, however, to stimulate successful collaborations. First, academic leaders must be cognizant of both the benefits and pitfalls of faculty collaboration. They should be aware of the specific problems that sometimes emerge in collaborative arrangements (disagreements over credit for authorship, exploitation of junior colleagues, for example) and be prepared to intervene whenever necessary to resolve them. Administrators should learn how to cultivate collaborative relationships among their faculty. Helping faculty to identify shared interests and define projects they can work on together is a prime way academic leaders can increase the level of collaboration among faculty. This type of liaison can be especially helpful to junior faculty, women, minorities, and other professors whose careers could benefit from collaboration with colleagues.

Another way academic leaders can promote collaboration is by helping faculty to present their collaborative activities and projects in the most advantageous manner. Consulting with professors on how they can effectively describe these activities to tenure and promotion committees can reinforce the value of investing time and effort in work where credit must be shared with other colleagues.

Administrators can reinforce the collaborative efforts of faculty in quiet but powerful ways. Brief notes acknowledging co-authored publications, grants shared with other colleagues, or good ratings on a team-taught course can boost the morale of professors. Similarly, casual conversations about the progress of a joint project or an invitation to lunch for an update on team research demonstrates that administrators are aware of professors' collaborative activities and care about their success. Attention of this sort costs very little but is a potent means of sustaining faculty collaboration.

Modeling collaborative behavior is perhaps the most compelling way for academic leaders to foster collaboration among faculty. Administrators who take the time to team teach or co-author articles explicitly convey their respect for collaborative work. By practicing what they preach, academic leaders demonstrate that collaboration can enhance productivity and enrich academic life.

Recommendations for Higher Education as a Field

1. *Create new structures to facilitate interaction and collaboration across typical boundaries that confine faculty.*

Many invisible but strong barriers in higher education inhibit faculty collaboration, limiting faculty interaction and confining many professors to narrow fields of study and a limited assortment of professional activities. Academic disciplines, rank, discrete types of institutions, even gender impose barriers on faculty.

The strong disciplinary cultures that structure higher education in the United States have facilitated many significant advances in knowledge and have provided a firm foundation for productive faculty careers. At the same time, they restrict professors' professional lives and their potential as teachers and scholars. Untenured faculty quickly get the message that they should limit their research and teaching to mainstream issues within the boundaries of their discipline if they wish to have a future in higher education.

Academic rank often keeps professors from interacting in a meaningful way. It is common, for example, for academic departments to reserve large introductory courses for junior faculty and small, upper-division courses for veteran professors. Such arrangements deter junior and senior faculty from working together to solve complex problems in teaching and research.

Similarly, society's perception of gender differences discourages men and women faculty from developing close working relationships. This barrier limits the opportunities for collaboration and the creative capacity of both sexes.

Higher education must find effective strategies to break down barriers inhibiting collaboration. Many of the problems that now confront Western civilization and humankind in general are too complex to be solved by independent scholars or single disciplines. These problems require multiple talents and often an interdisciplinary perspective that can be achieved only when intelligent people representing many fields of study pool their intellectual resources. In the same vein, research on faculty vitality (Baldwin 1990; Clark and Corcoran 1985) suggests that professors should not be confined to rigid, predetermined roles and career paths. Empirical evidence indicates that vital professors lead dynamic, diversified professional lives involving a wide range of interests, responsibilities, and, frequently, collaborations with colleagues. Higher education, which needs to play an increasingly important role in society, could be more creative and influential and take more risks if it learns better ways to make connections and supersede barriers that limit its ability to advance understanding and solve problems.

2. *Develop strategies to socialize students to collaboration in graduate school.*

At present, professors typically learn about collaboration haphazardly. Those fortunate enough to have a mentor or like-minded colleague learn to collaborate on the job. Many faculty, however, never find a professional partner and hence proceed solo through their careers. For higher education to reap maximum benefits from collaboration, students should learn about the collaborative process, gain an appreciation for it, and have opportunities to practice it as a formal part of their educational program. Collaborative learning is gaining widespread acceptance as an effective educational strategy. College students could learn to collaborate through regular opportunities to work together on papers and projects for courses. Student/faculty collaboration on research, writing, and instruction is another means to develop the skills and habits of effective teamwork. Finally, courses that engage students in collaborative activities should include explicit discussions of the collaborative process, its benefits, and its potential pitfalls so students can learn to judge when collaborative approaches to problems are most likely to be effective.

3. *Include in faculty development programs (especially for junior faculty) attention to the value and usefulness of collaborative work.*

Programs focusing on collaboration should discuss:

1. How to identify colleagues to work with,
2. How to initiate collaborative projects,
3. How to collaborate effectively, and
4. How to handle potential dysfunctions in collaborative relationships.

It is particularly appropriate to address issues of this sort in orientation programs for new faculty. Early identification of collaborative partners can ease the transition to an academic career and foster the productivity so critical to the success of probationary faculty.

4. Broaden the notion of successful faculty work and achievement.

A call for more collaboration by college and university faculty in no way diminishes the merits of individual teaching and scholarship. More faculty collaboration will not eliminate the work faculty do independently; rather, it will diversify and enrich professors' work lives. To achieve this beneficial outcome, however, the academic profession must expand its appreciation for collectively produced work. Conventional wisdom and the reward structure that currently pervade higher education often treat collaborative products as second class, if not deviant. The academic profession as a whole and many disciplines should rethink their emphasis on competition and autonomy and increase their appreciation for interdependence and complementarity. By acknowledging the value added to academic life through collaboration, higher education can strengthen its most valuable resource—the faculty.

Implications for Future Research
This monograph has discussed what is known about collaboration among faculty—about its benefits and potential problems, about who collaborates and under what circumstances, and about the process of doing productive collaborative work. Because the research and writing concerning collaboration specifically among faculty is fairly limited, this monograph also has drawn from that literature concerning teamwork and collaboration in other sectors that seemed illuminating to an understanding of collaboration among faculty. While the compilation of findings from the array of literature we have consulted provides a solid base of knowledge regarding collaboration among faculty, many questions remain unanswered. Answers to these questions would be helpful to administrators, faculty members, and institutions that wish to implement some of the recommendations advanced previously in this section. Additionally, scholars of higher education generally and the professoriate specifically could find some of the unan-

swered questions pertaining to faculty collaboration to be particularly challenging and interesting.

Throughout this monograph, collaboration among faculty has been approached as an interpersonal process (Aram and Morgan 1976) among individuals of different life and career stages and with diverse personal characteristics, occurring in an institutional and/or disciplinary context, for the purpose of pursuing goals together that would be more difficult, if not impossible, for faculty to achieve alone. Several elements of this approach to faculty collaboration stand out as useful rubrics by which to conceptualize a research agenda concerning collaboration among faculty. First, a set of issues and questions can be identified concerning the form and process of collaboration among faculty members. Second, the diversity of life, career, and personal issues that accompany faculty members who engage in collaborative work raise a variety of other important questions. Third, the fact that faculty members work within diverse institutional and disciplinary contexts suggests other questions whose answers could expand knowledge about collaboration among faculty. Fourth, potential research questions pertain to the outcomes and products of collaborative work. The research agenda presented here is organized around these four conceptual areas.

More faculty collaboration will not eliminate the work faculty do independently; rather, it will diversify and enrich professors' work lives.

Issues concerning the form and process of faculty collaboration

More needs to be known about the types and forms of collaboration in which faculty members engage. The following questions deserve particular study:

- What are the various kinds of collaborations that faculty members develop? What other forms does faculty collaboration take, in addition to the teamwork around research and around teaching that have been discussed in this volume? For example, to what extent are faculty members engaged in collaborative consulting activities?
- To what extent and in what ways are faculty members collaborating with individuals outside higher education? "Action research" in elementary or secondary schools or with public health or other social service agencies is an example. How are relationships between faculty members and others formed?

- What kinds of collaborative relationships are most productive and in what ways? For example, is it more beneficial when the collaborative partners are quite similar in interests, expertise, and work style, or when they are complementary?
- What are the differing advantages of long-term collaborations versus short-term collaborations?
- What are the distinctive differences between collaboration in higher education and collaboration in other sectors? Are there lessons or useful ideas faculty members could gain by learning more about the forms and processes of collaboration in other sectors?

The research in sectors other than higher education has focused more on the process of teamwork and collaboration than has the higher education literature. While a few articles can be cited, many intriguing questions remain concerning the process in which faculty members engage as they collaborate:

- How do those faculty who engage in collaboration find each other? How do they initiate their collaborative partnerships? What are effective strategies for finding colleagues with whom to collaborate and for initiating joint projects?
- How do collaborators terminate their partnerships? What are effective strategies for ending collaborations? Particularly, what are effective strategies for terminating problematic or unproductive collaborative relationships?
- What factors (personal, disciplinary, or organizational, among others) inhibit or preclude collaboration? What factors encourage or facilitate productive collaboration?
- How does the experience of collaboration differ depending on the status of the partners (for example, senior/junior, senior/senior, junior/junior teams)? What are the characteristics, benefits, and drawbacks of the different types of relationships?
- What is the process through which long-distance collaborations proceed (for example, scientists from different countries who communicate regularly by computer about their work)?
- How do various communication technologies (such as fax machines, electronic mail, and computers) affect collaborative practices?

- When collaboratively authored scholarly articles are compared, has the process of collaboration differed for those articles accepted for publication versus those rejected?

Issues concerning the individual dimensions of faculty collaboration

Faculty members who enter collaborative teams may play different roles; that is, not every member of a team participates in exactly the same way. Gender and other personal factors could relate to the different roles collaborators assume. Some important questions relate to this aspect:

- Within academic collaboration, what kind of roles or patterns of behavior do faculty members assume? Do certain role patterns or role arrangements in collaborative groups prove most effective?
- Are styles, roles, and behavior in collaboration associated with gender in particular ways? That is, do men and women differ in how they approach their part in a collaborative group? Why? Do collaborative interactions differ in single-sex compared to mixed-sex arrangements?
- To what extent and in what ways do minority faculty memers participate in collaboration? Might the building of collaborative relationships be a vehicle that contributes to the successful socialization of minority faculty members in the junior ranks?

Involvement in a collaborative project could hold different benefits and challenges for faculty members, depending on their career stage. Conversely, the kind of contributions faculty members can make to collaborative relationships can vary across the career stages. A variety of questions concerning the relationship between faculty career stages and collaboration invite study:

- How does socialization in graduate school affect faculty views of and abilities to engage in collaborative work? How might graduate schools better socialize and prepare doctoral students for collaboration?
- To what extent do the ways that faculty at different career stages experience and participate in collaboration vary? Should faculty members at all career stages be encouraged to collaborate?

- How do long-term collaborative relationships change over time? What advantages and what problems emerge after a collaborative team has worked together for some time?
- Can a profile of frequent faculty collaborators be developed? How are the careers of frequent collaborators affected by their collaborations? How do their careers differ from those who collaborate little or not at all?

Issues concerning the contexts for faculty collaboration

The institutional context within which a professor works could affect his or her experience with collaboration. For example, professors in liberal arts colleges might have considerable opportunity and encouragement to team teach but those working in major universities might not receive similar encouragement. Conversely, research collaboration may be more prevalent for university faculty but less likely for community college or liberal arts faculty (though this approach to research can be especially productive for faculty whose busy teaching schedules preclude substantial research time). The institutional context also can affect the extent and nature of faculty collaboration through policies and administrative practices. The following questions concerning the institutional climate as it relates to faculty collaboration would be fruitful to pursue:

- Does collaboration among faculty (the frequency and form) vary by institutional type?
- What institutions and administrative policies and practices facilitate collaboration? Which policies and practices inhibit collaboration?
- Do examples exist of institutions and administrators who successfully and consciously foster collaboration?
- Do student experiences and outcomes differ in institutions where faculty collaboration is highly valued?
- In what ways (if at all) do collaborative groups contribute to institutional effectiveness and success? Does collaboration affect the sense of community within a university or college?
- Do patterns of collaboration change as research facilities and equipment become more costly? Do patterns of collaboration differ in times of budgetary abundance from those of budgetary stringency?

Collaborative experiences and outcomes might differ not only across institutional contexts. Faculty members' disciplines and fields also form a context that affects how they approach collaboration:

- How do the process and form of collaboration vary across disciplines? What are the motivations that lead faculty members to collaborate in different fields? To what extent do faculty members in different fields bring varying assumptions and beliefs about collaboration to their work?
- In fields where collaboration is not frequent, what factors lead some faculty members to engage in this kind of work? What are the barriers that these faculty members face? How do they meet these barriers?
- In what ways do disciplinary and professional associations foster collaborative activity among faculty members? To what extent does the networking that occurs through professional and scholarly meetings lead to actual collaborative projects? How might associations further support faculty collaboration?

Issues concerning the outcomes of faculty collaboration

Based on the extant literature, this volume has argued that collaboration among faculty members offers many benefits. Yet much remains to be studied about the outcomes and products of faculty collaboration:

- How do faculty members in different fields perceive the outcomes (both positive and negative) of collaboration? How do deans and department chairs perceive the results of this form of faculty work?
- In what ways do the outcomes and benefits of different forms of collaboration vary? For example, do those who participate in teaching-related collaboration report different benefits from those reported by faculty who engage in research collaboration?
- Does collaboration enhance research productivity or, in contrast, do faculty members who already have a commitment and record of high research productivity choose to collaborate more frequently than their less productive colleagues?

- To what extent (if at all) does collaboration among academics result in increased risk taking and creativity and in increased satisfaction (as much of the literature on teamwork in other sectors suggests)?
- To what extent do faculty who engage in collaboration actually experience the potential ethical problems this volume has highlighted? Are ethical dilemmas more likely to occur in certain forms of collaboration (collaboration for research, for example, compared to teaching-related collaboration)?

Other research recommendations

Finally, in addition to identifying research questions whose answers will enrich our understanding of this important and potentially very fruitful kind of faculty work, we call for consideration of two particular approaches to the study of faculty collaboration. First, more *qualitative* study is needed concerning the process, experience, and impact of faculty collaboration. Most of the studies specifically concerning collaboration among faculty members are quantitative in design. Certainly, more quantitative work is necessary to answer this long research agenda. Because little qualitative work has been done, with its particular usefulness in focusing on the details and the complexity of a phenomenon, however, we urge special attention to some qualitative work in response to the research agenda. Second, longitudinal studies and ongoing data collection are needed. A deeper base of knowledge regarding the process and impact of collaboration for faculty members and their institutions requires not only isolated studies, but also long-term and continuing data collection and analysis.

Collaborative work among faculty members offers potentially rich benefits in terms of the production of knowledge and institutional quality, creativity and new perspectives, faculty growth and revitalization, and institutional excellence. We urge faculty members and administrative leaders, as well as scholars of higher education, to consider engaging in, supporting, and exploring more about this facet of professorial work.

REFERENCES

The Educational Resources Information Center (ERIC) Clearinghouse on Higher Education abstracts and indexes the current literature on higher education for inclusion in ERIC's data base and announcement in ERIC's monthly bibliographic journal, *Resources in Education* (RIE). Most of these publications are available through the ERIC Document Reproduction Service (EDRS). For publications cited in this bibliography that are available from EDRS, ordering number and price code are included. Readers who wish to order a publication should write to the ERIC Document Reproduction Service, 7420 Fullerton Rd., Suite 110, Springfield, VA 22153-2852. (Phone orders with VISA or MasterCard are taken at 800-443-ERIC or 703-440-1400.) When ordering, please specify the document (ED) number. Documents are available as noted in microfiche (MF) and paper copy (PC). If you have the price code ready when you call EDRS, an exact price can be quoted. The last page of the latest issue of *Resources in Education* also has the current cost, listed by code.

American Council on Education. 1988. *Minorities in Higher Education: Seventh Annual Status Report. 1988.* Washington, D.C.: Author. ED 320 509. 58 pp. MF–01; PC–03.

American Psychological Association. 1983. "Ethical Principles of Psychologists, Principle 7f." In *Publication Manual of the American Psychological Association,* 3d ed. Washington, D.C.: Author.

Aram, John D., and Cyril P. Morgan. 1976. "The Role of Project Team Collaboration in R&D Performance." *Management Science* 22(10): 1127–37.

Aram, John D., Cyril P. Morgan, and Edward S. Esbeck. 1971. "Relation of Collaborative Interpersonal Relationships to Individual Satisfaction and Organizational Performance." *Administrative Science Quarterly* 16: 289–96.

Argyris, C. 1964. *Integrating the Individual and the Organization.* New York: John Wiley & Sons.

Aronson, E. 1978. *The Jigsaw Classroom.* Beverly Hills, Cal.: Sage.

Austin, Ann E. 1990. "To Leave an Indelible Mark: Encouraging Good Teaching in Research Universities through Faculty Development." Unpublished report. Nashville: Vanderbilt Univ.

Baldwin, Roger G. March/April 1990. "Faculty Vitality beyond the Research University: Extending a Contextual Concept." *Journal of Higher Education* 61: 160–80.

Baum, William C., G.N. Griffiths, Robert Matthews, and Daniel Scherruble. 1976. "American Political Science before the Mirror: What Our Journals Reveal about the Profession." *Journal of Politics* 38: 895–917.

Bayer, Alan E., and John C. Smart. 1988. "Author Collaborative Styles in Academic Scholarship." Paper presented at an annual meeting of the American Educational Research Association, April, New Orleans, Louisiana.

Beaver, D.deB., and R. Rosen. 1978. "Studies in Scientific Collaboration, Part I: The Professional Origins of Scientific Co-Authorship." *Scientometrics* 1: 65–84.

———. 1979. "Studies in Scientific Collaboration, Part III." *Scientometrics* 1: 231–45.

Begum, K.J., and L.K. Sami. January 1988. "Research Collaboration in Agricultural Science." *International Library Review* 20: 57–63.

Belenky, M.F., B.M. Clinchy, N.R. Goldberger, and J.M. Tarule. 1986. *Women's Ways of Knowing.* New York: Basic Books.

Bennis, W.G. 1966. *Changing Organizations.* New York: McGraw-Hill.

Bennis, W.G., and H.A. Shepard. 1956. "A Theory of Group Development." *Human Relations* 9(4): 415–57.

Berelson, Bernard. 1960. *Graduate Education in the United States.* New York: McGraw-Hill.

Berger, R.A. 1986. "Private Sector Initiatives in the Reagan Administration." In *Public-Private Partnerships: Improving Urban Life,* edited by P. Davis. New York: Academy of Political Science.

Biglan, Anthony. June 1973. "The Characteristics of Subject Matter in Different Academic Areas." *Journal of Applied Psychology* 57: 195–203.

Birnbaum, Philip H. Summer 1981. "Academic Interdisciplinary Research: Characteristics of Successful Projects." *SRA Journal:* 5–16.

Blake, R., and J.S. Mouton. 1964. *The Managerial Grid.* Houston: Gulf.

Boice, Robert. 1990. "Mentoring New Faculty." *Journal of Staff, Program, and Organization* 8: 143–60.

———. 1992. "Lessons Learned about Mentoring." In *Developing New and Junior Faculty,* edited by M.D. Sorcinelli and A.E. Austin. New Directions in Teaching and Learning. San Francisco: Jossey-Bass. In press.

Boyer, Ernest L. 1990. *Scholarship Reconsidered: Priorities of the Professoriate.* Princeton, N.J.: Carnegie Foundation for the Advancement of Teaching. ED 326 149. 151 pp. MF–01; PC not available EDRS.

Brady, Laura A. 1988. "Collaborative Literary Writing: Issues of Authorship and Authority." Ph.D. dissertation, Univ. of Minnesota.

Bridgwater, Carol Austin, Philip H. Bornstein, and John Walkenbach. 1980. "Assigning Publication Credit in Collaborative Research." Paper presented at a meeting of the American Psychological Association, September, Montreal, Quebec, Canada. ED 194 841. 11 pp. MF–01; PC–01.

———. May 1981. "Ethical Issues and the Assignment of Publication Credit." *American Psychologist* 36: 524–25.

Bruffee, Kenneth A. November 1984. "Collaborative Learning and the 'Conversation of Mankind.'" *College English* 46: 635–52.

———. December 1986. "Social Construction, Language, and the

Authority of Knowledge: A Bibliographic Essay." *College English* 48: 773–90.

———. March/April 1987. "The Art of Collaborative Learning." *Change:* 42–47.

Cameron, Don. March 1984. "Against Collaboration." *Arts Magazine* 58(7): 83–87.

Cameron, Susan W., and Robert T. Blackburn. July/August 1981. "Sponsorship and Academic Career Success." *Journal of Higher Education* 52: 369–77.

Choi, Jin M. 1988. "An Analysis of Authorship in Anthropology Journals, 1963 and 1983." *Behavioral and Social Sciences Librarian* 6: 85–94.

Clark, Shirley M., and Mary Corcoran. 1985. "Individual and Organizational Contributions to Faculty Vitality: An Institutional Case Study." In *Faculty Vitality and Institutional Productivity: Perspectives for Higher Education,* edited by Shirley M. Clark and Darrell R. Lewis. New York: Teachers College Press.

Cohen, Bernard P., Ronald J. Kruse, and Michael Anbar. April 1982. "The Social Structure of Scientific Research Teams." *Pacific Sociological Review* 25(2): 205–32.

Cole, Jonathan R., and Harriet Zuckerman. 1984. "The Productivity Puzzle: Persistence and Change in Patterns of Publication of Men and Women Scientists." *Advances in Motivation and Achievement* 2: 217–58.

Cooper, Jim, and Randall Mueck. 1990. "Student Involvement in Learning: Cooperative Learning and College Instruction." *Journal of Excellence in College Teaching* 1: 68–76.

Cosner, Lewis A. 1965. *Men of Ideas.* New York: Free Press.

Cummings, T.G. 1984. "Transorganizational Development." In *Research in Organizational Behavior,* vol. 6, edited by B. Stow and L. Cummings. Greenwich, Conn.: JAI Press.

Dailey, Robert C. November 1978. "The Role of Team and Task Characteristics in R&D Team Collaborative Problem Solving and Productivity." *Management Science* 24: 1579–88.

Daniels, Craig E. 1984. "Integrated Cluster of Independent Courses: An Ideal Curricular Cluster." *Innovative Higher Education* 8(2): 115–23.

Davis, P. 1986. "Why Partnerships: Why Now?" In *Public-Private Partnerships: Improving Urban Life,* edited by P. Davis. New York: Academy of Political Science.

Day, R., and J.V. Day. 1977. "A Review of the Current State of Negotiated Order Theory: An Appreciation and a Critique." *Sociological Quarterly* 18: 126–42.

Dimancescu, D., and J. Botlein. 1986. *The New Alliance: America's R&D Consortia.* Cambridge, Mass.: Ballinger.

DuBois, Ellen Carol, Gail Paradise Kelly, Elizabeth Lapovsky Kennedy, Carolyn W. Korsmeyer, and Lillian S. Robinson. 1985. *Feminist*

Scholarship: Kindling in the Groves of Academe. Chicago: Univ. of Chicago Press.

Duckworth, M., and T.L. Lowe. 1986. "Physics and Speech Therapy." *Physics Education* 21: 74–79.

Dunlop, J.T. 1 June 1987. "Alternative Means of Dispute Resolution in Government." Working Paper. Cambridge, Mass.: Harvard Univ.

Dyer, W.G. 1987. *Team Building: Issues and Alternatives.* Reading, Mass.: Addison-Wesley.

Easterby-Smith, Mark, and Nils-Goran Olve. 1984. "Team Teaching: Making Management Education More Student-Centered?" *Management Education and Development* 15(3): 221–36.

Eaton, Joseph W. 1951. "Social Processes of Professional Teamwork." *American Sociological Review* 16: 707–13.

Elliott, J. 1981. "Action Research: A Framework for Self-Evaluation in Schools." TIQL Working Paper No. 1. Cambridge, Eng.: Cambridge Institute of Education.

Farris, G. 1973. "Leadership and Supervision in the Informal Organization." Working Paper No. 665-73. Cambridge, Mass.: Alfred P. Sloan School of Management.

Fennell, Mary L., and Gary D. Sandefur. 1983. "Structural Clarity of Interdisciplinary Teams: A Research Note." *Journal of Applied Behavioral Science* 19(2): 193–202.

Finkelstein, Martin J. 1984. *The American Academic Profession: A Synthesis of Social Scientific Inquiry Since World War II.* Columbus: Ohio State Univ. Press.

Flanagan, Michael F., and David A. Ralston. 1983. "Intra-Coordinated Team Teaching: Benefits for Both Students and Instructors." *Teaching of Psychology* 10(2): 116–17.

Fowler, Susan L., and David Roeger. December 1986. "Programmer and Writer Collaboration: Making User Manuals that Work." *IEEE Transactions on Professional Communications* 29(4): 21–25.

Fox, Mary F. 1985a. "Publication, Performance, and Reward in Science and Scholarship." In *Higher Education: Handbook of Theory and Research,* vol. 1, edited by John Smart. New York: Agathon Press.

———. 1985b. "The Transition from Dissertation Student to Publishing Scholar and Professional." In *Scholarly Writing and Publishing: Issues, Problems, and Solutions,* edited by Mary F. Fox. Boulder, Colo.: Westview Press.

Fox, Mary Frank, and Catherine A. Faver. July 1982. "The Process of Collaboration in Scholarly Research." *Scholarly Publishing* 13: 327–39.

———. May/June 1984. "Independence and Cooperation in Research: The Motivations and Costs of Collaboration." *Journal of Higher Education* 55(3): 347–59.

Frierson, Henry T. 1990. "The Situation of Black, Educational Researchers: Continuation of a Crisis." *Educational Researcher* 19(2): 12–17.

Fuchs, Gordon E., and Louise P. Moore. 1988. "Collaboration for Understanding and Effectiveness." *Clearing House* 61: 410–13.

Garza, Hisauro. 1988. "The 'Barriorization' of Hispanic Faculty." *Educational Record* 69(1): 122–24.

Gaventa, John. 1980. *Power and Powerlessness: Quiescence and Rebellion in an Appalachian Valley.* Urbana: Univ. of Illinois Press.

Gebhardt, Richard. 1980. "Teamwork and Feedback: Broadening the Base of Collaborative Writing." *College English* 42(1): 69–75.

George, Paul S. November 1987. "Training: Team Building without Teams." *Personnel Journal:* 122–29.

Geyman, John P., and James A. Deyrup. 1984. "Subgroup Report on Teamwork Skills." *Journal of Medical Education* 59: 169–72.

Gibson, Gregory L. 1987. "Multiple Authorship in the *Journal of Personality and Social Psychology,* 1965–1986: Probable Causes, Possible Effects." Doctoral dissertation, Brigham Young Univ.

Gillespie, David F., and Philip H. Birnbaum. 1980. "Status Concordance, Coordination, and Success in Interdisciplinary Research Teams." *Human Relations* 33: 41–56.

Goffman, E. 1983. "The Interaction Order." *American Sociological Review* 48: 1–17.

Gordon, M.D. 1980. "A Critical Assessment of Inferred Relations between Multiple Authorship, Scientific Collaboration, the Production of Papers, and Their Acceptance for Publication." *Scientometrics* 2: 193–201.

Granovetter, M. 1973. "The Strength of Weak Ties." *American Journal of Sociology* 78: 1360–80.

Gray, B. 1985. "Conditions Facilitating Interorganizational Collaboration." *Human Relations* 38(10): 911–36.

———. 1989. *Collaborating: Finding Common Ground for Multiparty Problems.* San Francisco: Jossey-Bass.

Griffith, Belver C., and Nicholas C. Mullins. 15 September 1972. "Coherent Social Groups in Scientific Change." *Science* 177: 959–64.

Grinnell, S.K. 1969. "The Informal Action Group: One Way to Collaborate in a University." *Journal of Applied Behavioral Science* 5(1): 75–103.

Grundy, S., and S. Kemmis. 1982. "Educational Action Research in Australia: The State of the Art." In *The Action Research Reader.* Victoria, Australia: Deakin Univ.

Hagstrom, Warren O. 1964. "Traditional and Modern Forms of Scientific Teamwork." *Administrative Science Quarterly* 9: 241–63.

———. 1965. *The Scientific Community.* New York: Basic Books.

Hall, Gene E. 1976. "Longitudinal and Cross-Sectional Studies of the Concerns of Users of Team Teaching in the Elementary School and Instructional Modules at the College Level." Austin, Tex.: Research and Development Center for Teacher Education. ED 251 428. 19 pp. MF–01; PC–01.

Hamel, Gary, Yoes L. Doz, and C.K. Prahalad. January/February 1989. "Collaborate with Your Competitors—and Win." *Harvard Business Review:* 133–39.

Hargens, L.L. 1975. *Patterns of Scientific Research.* Washington, D.C.: American Sociological Association.

Hawking, Stephen W. 1988. *A Brief History of Time: From the Big Bang to Black Holes.* New York: Bantam Books.

Heath, David A., Nancy Carlson, and Daniel Kurtz. 1987. "Team Teaching Optometry." *Journal of Optometric Education* 12(3): 76–80.

Heffner, Alan G. 1979. "Authorship Recognition of Subordinates in Collaborative Research." *Social Studies of Science* 9: 377–84.

Heil, Lillian. 1986. "A University Faculty Member's Perspective: Lesson Learned from a Partnership Experience." Paper presented at the annual meeting of the American Educational Research Association, April, San Francisco, California. ED 274 301. 9 pp. MF–01; PC–01.

Helgesen, Sally. 1990. *The Female Advantage: Women's Ways of Leadership.* New York: Doubleday Currency.

Holmes, Zoe A. May 1989. "Roles and Attitudes of Authors Regarding Multiple Authorship of Papers in *Journal of Food Science.*" *Food Technology* 43: 94–108.

Hood, Jane C. 1985. "The Lone Scholar Myth." In *Scholarly Writing and Publishing: Issues, Problems, and Solutions,* edited by Mary F. Fox. Boulder, Colo.: Westview Press.

Hord, S.M. 1981. "Working Together: Cooperation or Collaboration." Austin: Univ. of Texas at Austin, Research and Development Center for Teacher Education. ED 226 450. 21 pp. MF–01; PC–01.

Huston, Mary M., and Willie Parson. Spring 1985. "A Model of Librarianship for Combining Learning and Teaching." *Research Strategies* 3(2): 75–80.

Isenberg, Joan P., Mary Renck Jalongo, and Karen D'Angelo Bromley. 1987. "The Role of Collaboration in Scholarly Writing: A National Study." Paper presented at the annual meeting of the American Educational Research Association, April, Washington, D.C. ED 287 873. 43 pp. MF–01; PC–02.

Johnson, David W., and Roger T. Johnson. 1975. *Learning Together and Alone.* Englewood Cliffs, N.J.: Prentice-Hall.

———. 1983. "The Socialization and Achievement Crisis: Are Cooperative Learning Experiences the Solution?" In *Applied Social Psychology Annual 4,* edited by L. Bickman. Beverly Hills, Cal.: Sage.

———. November 1987. "Research Shows the Benefits of Adult Cooperation." *Educational Leadership* 45: 27–30.

Johnson, David W., Roger T. Johnson, and Karl A. Smith. 1991a. *Active Learning: Cooperation in the College Classroom.* Edina, Minn.: Interaction Book Co.

———. 1991b. *Cooperative Learning: Increasing College Faculty Instructional Productivity.* ASHE-ERIC Higher Education Report No. 4. Washington, D.C.: George Washington Univ., School of Education and Human Development.

Johnson, David W., Geoffrey Maruyama, Roger Johnson, Deborah Nelson, and Linda Skon. 1981. "Effects of Cooperative, Competitive, and Individualistic Goal Structures on Achievement: A Meta-Analysis." *Psychological Bulletin* 89: 47–62.

Kanter, Rosabeth M. 1977. *Men and Women of the Corporation*. New York: Basic Books.

———. 1983. *The Change Masters*. New York: Simon & Schuster.

Katz, Joseph, and Mildred Henry. 1988. *Turning Professors into Teachers: A New Approach to Faculty Development and Student Learning*. New York: ACE/Macmillan.

Kaufman, Debra R. 1978. "Associational Ties in Academe: Some Male and Female Differences." *Sex Roles* 4: 9–21.

Kemmis, S., and R. McTaggart. 1982. *The Action Research Planner*. Victoria, Australia: Deakin Univ.

Keohane, Nannerl O. Spring 1985. "Collaboration and Leadership: Are They in Conflict?" *College Board Review* 135: 4–6.

Kohn, Alfie. 1986. *No Contest: The Case against Competition*. Boston: Houghton Mifflin.

Kornbluth, Jesse. October 1987. "I Was a CEO Ghost." *Across the Board* 24(10): 51–54.

Kuhn, Thomas S. 1970. *The Structure of Scientific Revolutions*. 2d ed. Chicago: Univ. of Chicago Press.

Kyle, Diane W., and Gail McCutcheon. 1984. "Collaborative Research: Development and Issues." *Journal of Curriculum Studies* 16(2): 173–79.

LaFauci, Horatio M., and Peyton E. Richter. 1970. *Team Teaching at the College Level*. New York: Pergamon Press.

Lawler, E.E., III. 1986. *High-Involvement Management: Participative Strategies for Improving Organizational Performance*. San Francisco: Jossey-Bass.

Lewin, K. 1948. *Resolving Social Conflicts*. New York: Harper & Brothers.

———. 1951. *Field Theory in Social Science*. New York: Harper & Row.

Likert, R. 1961. *New Patterns of Management*. New York: McGraw-Hill.

Lindsey, Duncan. 1980. "Production and Citation Measures in the Sociology of Science: The Problem of Multiple Authorship." *Social Studies of Science* 10: 145–62.

Little, J.W. 1981. "School Success and Staff Development in Urban Desegregated Schools: A Summary of Recently Completed Research." Paper presented at an annual meeting of the American Educational Research Association, April, Los Angeles, California. ED 205 628. 27 pp. MF–01; PC–02.

Lobb, M. Delbert. 1964. *Practical Aspects of Team Teaching*. San Francisco: Fearon Publishers.

Lordahl, Janice B., and Gerald Gordon. February 1972. "The Structure of Scientific Fields and the Functioning of University Graduate Departments." *American Sociological Review* 37: 57–72.

Lynton, Ernest A., and Sandra E. Elman. 1987. *New Priorities for the University: Meeting Society's Needs for Applied Knowledge and Competent Individuals.* San Francisco: Jossey-Bass.

McCabe, Cynthia J. 1984. "Artistic Collaboration in the Twentieth Century: The Period between Two Wars." In *Artistic Collaboration in the Twentieth Century,* edited by C.J. McCabe. Washington, D.C.: Smithsonian Institution Press.

McCadden, Joseph F. January 1983. "Team-Teaching: Quality Circles for Teachers." *Innovation Abstracts* 5(1).

McCann, J.E. 1983. "Design Guidelines for Social Problem-Solving Interventions." *Journal of Applied Behavioral Science* 19: 177–89.

McGregor, D.M. 1960. *The Human Side of Enterprise.* New York: McGraw-Hill.

MacGregor, Jean. 1987. "Intellectual Development of Students in Learning Communities." Washington Center Occasional Paper No. 1. Olympia, Wash.: Evergreen State College.

———. 1990. "Collaboration Learning: Shared Inquiry as a Process of Reform." In *The Changing Face of College Teaching,* edited by Marilla D. Svinicki. New Directions for Teaching and Learning. San Francisco: Jossey-Bass.

McLaughlin, M.W., and D.D. Marsh. 1978. "Staff Development and School Change." *Teachers College Record* 80(1): 69–84.

Marquis, Donald G. 1963. Working Paper. Cambridge: Massachusetts Institute of Technology, Organizational Research Program.

Meadows, A.J. 1974. *Communication in Science.* London: Butterworths.

Moore, William, and Lonnie Wagstaff. 1974. *Black Educators in White Colleges.* San Francisco: Jossey-Bass.

Morlock, Henry C., William P. Goeddert, Naomi B. McCormick, Matthew R. Merrens, Lary C. Shaffer, and Taher Zandi. October 1988. "A Rotational Format for Team Teaching Introductory Psychology." *Teaching of Psychology* 15(3): 144–45.

Mulford, C.L., and D.L. Rogers. 1982. "Definitions and Models." In *Interorganizational Coordination,* edited by D.L. Rogers and D.A. Whetten. Ames: Iowa State Univ. Press.

Narin, F. 1976. *Evaluative Bibliometrics: The Use of Publication and Citation Analysis in the Evaluation of Scientific Activity.* Cherry Hill, N.J.: Computer Horizons.

Nicodemus, Robert. Fall 1984. "Lessons from a Course Team." *Teaching at a Distance* 25: 33–39.

Nobel, Darla R. 1986. "The Interaction of Task Type and Social Structure in Small Groups: An Analysis of Success in Interdisciplinary Research Teams." Ph.D. dissertation, Stanford Univ.

Obert, S. 1983. "Developmental Patterns of Organizational Task Groups: A Preliminary Study." *Human Relations* 36(1): 37–52.

O'Brien, Eileen M. 1990. "The Revolving Door Syndrome: Minority, Women Faculty Discuss Campus Climate." *Black Issues in Higher Education* 7(19): 1+.

Office of the Assistant Provost for Lifelong Education. March 1990. "Pioneering the Land-Grant University for the 21st Century." East Lansing: Michigan State Univ.

Oja, S.N., and G.J. Pine. 1981. *A Two-Year Study of Teacher Stages of Development in Relation to Collaborative Action Research on Schools.* Washington, D.C.: National Institute of Education Research. ED 248 227. 829 pp. MF–05; PC–34.

Oja, Sharon Nodie, and Lisa Smulyan. 1989. *Collaborative Action Research: A Developmental Approach.* New York: Falmer Press.

Oromaner, Mark. 1975. "Collaboration and Impact: The Career of Multiauthored Publications." *Social Science Information* 14: 147–55.

O'Rourke, Thomas W. March 1989. "The Student-Professor Relationship." *Journal of School Health* 59: 101–2.

Ouchi, William G. 1984. *The M-Form Society: How American Teamwork Can Recapture the Competitive Edge.* Reading, Mass.: Addison-Wesley.

Over, Ray. September 1982. "Collaborative Research and Publication in Psychology." *American Psychologist* 37: 996–1001.

Over, Ray, and Susan Smallman. February 1973. "Maintenance of Individual Visibility in Publication of Collaborative Research by Psychologists." *American Psychologist* 28: 161–66.

Palmer, Parker J. 1983. *To Know as We Are Known: A Spirituality of Education.* New York: Harper & Row.

Parker, Glenn M. 1990. *Team Players and Teamwork.* San Francisco: Jossey-Bass.

Patel, Narsi. 1973. "Collaboration in the Professional Growth of American Sociology." *Social Science Information* 12: 77–92.

Pelz, Donald C., and Frank M. Andrews. 1966. *Scientists in Organizations: Productive Climates for Research and Development.* New York: John Wiley & Sons.

Peters, T. 1987. *Thriving on Chaos.* New York: Alfred A. Knopf.

Peterson, Susan. 1990. "Challenges for Black Women Faculty." *Initiatives* 53: 1.

Plotnicov, Leonard. 1985. "Introducing Contemporary Anthropology: A Team-Taught Course for Large Classes." *Anthropology and Education Quarterly* 16: 256–60.

Pokorni, Judith, Helen Vojna, and Sylvia Carter. Spring 1982. "Training Manual for Local Head Start Staff: Part II." College Park, Md.: Head Start Resource and Training Center.

Polos, Nicholas. 1965. *The Dynamics of Team Teaching.* Dubuque, Iowa: Wm. C. Braun Co.

Port, Otis, with Zachary Schiller and Resa W. King. 30 April 1990. "A Smarter Way to Manufacture." *Business Week:* 110–13+.

Presser, Stanley. 1980. "Collaboration and the Quality of Research." *Social Studies of Science* 10: 95–101.

Quinn, Sandra L., and Sanford B. Kanter. December 1984. "Team Teaching: An Alternative to Lecture Fatigue." *Innovation Abstracts* 6(34).

Reagor, S., and W.S. Brown. 1978. "The Application of Advanced Technology to Scholarly Communication in the Humanities." *Computers and the Humanities* 12: 237–46.

Rice, R. Eugene, and Sandra I. Cheldelin. 1989. "The Knower and the Known: Making the Connection." Evaluation of the New Jersey Master Faculty Program. Unpublished report to the New Jersey Institute of Collegiate Teaching and Learning. South Orange, N.J.: Seton Hall Univ.

Rinn, Fauneil J., and Sybil B. Weir. Winter 1984. "Yea, Team." *Improving College and University Teaching* 32(1): 5–10.

Saunders, H.H. 1985. "We Need a Larger Theory of Negotiation: The Importance of Prenegotiating Phases." *Negotiation Journal* 1(3): 249–62.

Schechter, Patricia, Kwok Pui-lan, Margaret R. Miles, Renita J. Weems, and Majorie Suchochi. Spring 1987. "Roundtable Discussion: A Vision of Feminist Religious Scholarship." *Journal of Feminist Studies in Religion* 3(1): 91–111.

Schein, E. 1969. *Process Consultation: Its Role in Organizational Development.* Reading, Mass.: Addison-Wesley.

Schutz, W.C. 1958. *FIRO: A Three-Dimensional Theory of Interpersonal Behavior.* New York: Rinehart.

Seaman, Don F. 1981. *Working Effectively with Task-Oriented Groups.* New York: McGraw-Hill.

Shapiro, David. 1984. "Art as Collaboration: Toward a Theory of Pluralist Aesthetics, 1950–1980." In *Artistic Collaboration in the Twentieth Century,* edited by Cynthia J. McCabe. Washington, D.C.: Smithsonian Institution Press.

Sharan, S., and Y. Sharan. 1976. *Small-Group Teaching.* Englewood Cliffs, N.J.: Educational Technology Publications.

Shawchuck, Carita R., Michael Fatis, and Joseph L. Breitenstein. 1986. "A Practical Guide to the Assignment of Authorship Credit." *Behavior Therapist* 9: 216–17.

Shepard, H.A. 1965. "Changing Interpersonal and Intergroup Relationships in Organizations." In *Handbook of Organizations,* edited by J.G. March. Chicago: Rand McNally.

Shreeve, William, Janet R. Norby, Arnold F. Stueckle, William G.J. Goetter, Barbara deMichele, and Thomas K. Midgeley. Fall 1986. " '. . . If You Don't Care Who Gets the Credit.' " *Journal of the College and University Personnel Association* 37: 20–22.

Shulman, Judith. January 1988. "Look to a Colleague." *Instructor* 97:32-34.

Simeone, Angela. 1987. *Academic Women: Working towards Equality.* South Hadley, Mass.: Bergin & Garvey Publishers.

Simpson, Isaiah. Winter 1987. "Training and Evaluating Teaching Assistants through Team Teaching." *Freshman English News* 15(3): 4+.

Slavin, R.E. 1980. *Using Student Team Learning.* Rev. ed. Baltimore: Johns Hopkins Univ., Center for Social Organization of Schools.

———. 1983. "When Does Cooperative Learning Increase Student Achievement?" *Psychological Bulletin* 94: 429-45.

Smart, John C., and Alan E. Bayer. 1986. "Author Collaboration and Impact: A Note on Citation Rates of Single- and Multiple-Authored Articles." *Scientometrics* 10: 297-305.

Smith, Clagett G. December 1971. "Scientific Performance and the Composition of Research Teams." *Administrative Science Quarterly* 16: 486-95.

Spencer, Mary L., and Eva Bradford. 1982. "Status and Needs of Women Scholars." In *Handbook for Women Scholars,* edited by Mary L. Spencer, Monika Kehoe, and Karen Speece. San Francisco: American Behavioral Research Corp.

Spiegel, Don, and Patricia Keith-Spiegel. 1970. "Assignment of Publication Credits: Ethics and Practices of Psychologists." *American Psychologist* 25: 738-47.

Srivastva, S., S. Obert, and E. Neilson. 1977. "Organizational Analysis through Group Processes: A Theoretical Perspective for Organization Development." In *Organizational Development in the UK and USA,* edited by C. Cooper. London: Macmillan.

Stone, Sue. December 1982. "Progress in Documentation: Humanities Scholars' Information Needs and Uses." *Journal of Documentation* 38: 292-313.

Strauss, Anselm, Leonard Schatzman, Danuta Ehrlich, Rue Bucher, and Melvin Sabshin. 1963. "The Hospital and Its Negotiated Order." In *The Hospital in Modern Society,* edited by Eliot Freidson. New York: Free Press.

Strauss, D. 1978. *Negotiations: Varieties, Contexts, Processes, and Social Order.* San Francisco: Jossey-Bass.

Susskind, L., and D. Madigan. 1984. "New Approaches to Resolving Disputes in the Public Sector." *Justice System Journal* 9(2): 197-203.

Tannahill, Andrew, and Graham Robertson. 1986. "Health Education in Medical Education." *Medical Teacher* 8(2): 165-69.

Teghtsoonian, M. 1974. "Distribution by Sex of Authors and Editors of Psychological Journals, 1970-1972: Are There Enough Women Editors?" *American Psychologist* 29: 262-69.

Tims, Betty J. 1988. "Interactive Team Teaching of Government Documents Data Sources: A Case Study." *RSR—Reference Services*

Review 16(3): 69–72.

Tomlinson, Patricia S., Joyce A. Semradek, and Sherry T. Boyd. September/October 1986. "Programmatic Research: A Collaborative Model." *Journal of Professional Nursing* 2: 309–17.

Trist, E.L. 1983. "Referent Organizations and the Development of Interorganizational Domains." *Human Relations* 36(3): 247–68.

Tuckman, B.W. 1965. "Developmental Sequence in Small Groups." *Psychological Bulletin* (63)6: 384–89.

Tuckman, B.W., and M.C. Jensen. 1977. "Stages of Small-Group Development Revisited." *Group and Organization Studies* 2(4): 419–27.

Wallat, C., J.L. Green, S.M. Conlin, and M. Haramis. 1981. "Issues Related to Action Research in the Classroom—The Teacher and Researcher as a Team." In *Ethnography and Language in Educational Settings,* edited by J.L. Green and C. Wallat. Norwood, N.J.: Ablex.

Ware, Mark E., Louis E. Gardner, and Daniel P. Murphy. 1978. "Team Teaching Introductory Psychology as Pedagogy and for Faculty Development." *Teaching of Psychology* 5(3): 127–30.

Warwick, David. 1971. *Team Teaching.* London: Univ of London Press.

Weinberg, Armin D. March 1989. "Issues in Joint Authorship." *Journal of School Health* 59: 102–3.

Whipple, William R. October 1987. "Collaborative Learning: Recognizing It When We See It." *AAHE Bulletin* 40: 3–5. ED 289 396. 6 pp. MF–01; PC–01.

White, K.D., L. Dalgleish, and G. Arnold. 1982. "Authorship Patterns in Psychology: National and International Trends." *Bulletin of the Psychonomic Society* 20: 190–92.

"Who Needs a Boss?" 7 May 1990. *Fortune:* 52–60.

Wildavsky, Aaron. Spring 1986. "On Collaboration." *PS* 19: 237–48.

Wilkie, J.R., and I.L. Allen. 1975. "Women Sociologists and Co-Authorships with Men." *American Sociologist* 10: 19–24.

Wong, Herbert Y., and Jimy M. Sanders. January 1983. "Gender Differences in the Attainment of Doctorates." *Sociological Perspectives* 26: 29–50.

Zander, Alvin. 1979. "The Psychology of Group Processes." *Annual Review of Psychology* 30: 417–51.

Zuckerman, Harriet. 1968. "Patterns of Name Ordering among Authors of Scientific Papers: A Study of Symbolism and Its Ambiguity." *American Journal of Sociology* 74: 276–91.

Zuckerman, Harriet, and Jonathan R. Cole. Spring 1975. "Women in American Science." *Minerva* 13: 82–102.

Zuckerman, Harriet, and R.K. Merton. 1972. "Age, Aging, and Age Structure in Science." In *Aging and Society.* Vol. 3, *Sociology of Age Stratification,* edited by M.W. Riley, M. Johnson, and A. Foner. New York: Sage.

INDEX

A

Academic collaboration, 5
Academic evaluation and reward, 70
Academic life, 7
Academic reward system, 29
Action Community on Collaborative learning, 14
Action research, 22
Administrators and collaboration, 86
African-American faculty, 78
American Association for Higher Education, 14
American Psychological Association, 68
Anthropology
    archeological, 27
    biophysical, 27
    linguistic, 28
    sociocultural, 28
Astronomy
    observational, 27
    theoretical, 27
AT&T, 13
Authorship
    criteria, 69, 70
    disputes, 68
    patterns men and women, 78
    problems, 72
    recognition, 67
    relative contributions, 69, 71
    seniority, 69
    status, 72

B

Barriers to collaboration, 88
Business sector
    complementarity, 11
    interdependence, 11
    teamwork, 11

C

California, University of, Santa Barbara, 75, 76
Chemists
    collaboration, 30
    scholarly productivity, 30
Clemens, Samuel, 27
Citations, 32
Cluster courses, 39
Co-authorship
    exclusion, 77
Cohesiveness
    collaborative groups, 61, 62

Cooperative learning, 16
     effects, 17
     groups, 16
Costs of collaboration, 28
Creativity, 2
Cross sex relationships, 77

D

Dewey, 15
Division of labor, 64
Doctorates
     African-Americans, 78

E

Editorial collaboration, 23
Effective collaboration
     factors in, 55
Environment, 12

F

Faculty collaboration
     choice of colleagues, 63
     context, 94, 95
     form and process, 91
     individual dimensions, 93
     inhibition, 88
     issues, 91
     outcomes, 95
     steps in, 63
Faculty development, 89
Faculty morale, 33, 34
Feminist theory, 15
Ford, Ford Maddox, 27
Future research, 90
     implications for, 90, 91

G

General Motors
     Saturn plant, 13
Generalist teams, 37
Graduate students
     collaboration, 80
     exploitation, 80
Great Books programs, 15
Group dynamics, 49
     research, 50
     theories, 50
Group interaction, 50

Mature disciplines, 24
Minorities
        collaboration, 78
Minority faculty
        collaboration, 79
Mixed-gender groups, 62
Modelling collaborative behavior, 87
Models
        collaborative teaching, 36
Multiauthor publications, 25
Multiple authorship, 23

N

Natural sciences, 26
NCR, 13
Negotiated order theory, 48
New Jersey Institute for Collegiate Teaching and Learning, 40
New York, University of, 15
Nobel Prizes, 1

O

Old boy networks, 76

P

Performance improvement, 7
Perkins, Maxwell, 27
Physical sciences
        collaboration, 25
Piaget, 15
Problem solving
        collaborative, 30
        creative, 33
Productivity increase, 12
Professional connections
        quality of, 76
Professional identity, 29
Professional productivity, 8
Professional subordinates, 79
Professional work
        accountability, 73
Professionalization
        science, 6
Promoting collaborative activity, 87
Protege relationships
        senior faculty, 76
Psychological journals, 28
Publication credit, 68
Publication statistics, 31

R

S

T

practicalities, 53
process, 92
Technological change, 12
Termination of collaboration, 65
Type A teamwork, 22
Type C teamwork, 21
Type D teamwork, 22

U
Understanding collaboration, 85
Universalism, 68

W
Warner, Charles Dudley, 27
Wolfe, Thomas, 27
Women
collaboration, 74
collegial relationships, 75
graduate students, 76
networks, 76
Women academics
unmarried, 77
Women's Ways of Knowing, 75
Work guidelines, 65
Work teams, 33

ASHE-ERIC HIGHER EDUCATION REPORTS

Since 1983, the Association for the Study of Higher Education (ASHE) and the Educational Resources Information Center (ERIC) Clearinghouse on Higher Education, a sponsored project of the School of Education and Human Development at The George Washington University, have cosponsored the *ASHE-ERIC Higher Education Report* series. The 1991 series is the twentieth overall and the third to be published by the School of Education and Human Development at the George Washington University.

Each monograph is the definitive analysis of a tough higher education problem, based on thorough research of pertinent literature and institutional experiences. Topics are identified by a national survey. Noted practitioners and scholars are then commissioned to write the reports, with experts providing critical reviews of each manuscript before publication.

Eight monographs (10 before 1985) in the ASHE-ERIC Higher Education Report series are published each year and are available on individual and subscription bases. Subscription to eight issues is $90.00 annually; $70 to members of AAHE, AIR, or AERA; and $60 to ASHE members. All foreign subscribers must include an additional $10 per series year for postage.

To order single copies of existing reports, use the order form on the last page of this book. Regular prices, and special rates available to members of AAHE, AIR, AERA and ASHE, are as follows:

Series	Regular	Members
1990 and 91	$17.00	$12.75
1988 and 89	15.00	11.25
1985 to 87	10.00	7.50
1983 and 84	7.50	6.00
before 1983	6.50	5.00

Price includes book rate postage within the U.S. For foreign orders, please add $1.00 per book. Fast United Parcel Service available within the contiguous U.S. at $2.50 for each order under $50.00, and calculated at 5% of invoice total for orders $50.00 or above.

All orders under $45.00 must be prepaid. Make check payable to ASHE-ERIC. For Visa or MasterCard, include card number, expiration date and signature. A bulk discount of 10% is available on orders of 10 or more books, and 40% on orders of 25 or more books (not applicable on subscriptions).

Address order to
ASHE-ERIC Higher Education Reports
The George Washington University
1 Dupont Circle, Suite 630
Washington, DC 20036
Or phone (202) 296-2597
Write or call for a complete catalog.

1991 ASHE-ERIC Higher Education Reports

1. Active Learning: Creating Excitement in the Classroom
   Charles C. Bonwell and James A. Eison

2. Realizing Gender Equality in Higher Education: The Need to Integrate Work/Family Issues
   Nancy Hensel

3. Academic Advising for Student Success: A System of Shared Responsibility
   by Susan H. Frost

4. Cooperative Learning: Increasing College Faculty Instructional Productivity
   by David W. Johnson, Roger T. Johnson, and Karl A. Smith

5. High School–College Partnerships: Conceptual Models, Programs, and Issues
   by Arthur Richard Greenberg

6. Meeting the Mandate: Renewing the College and Departmental Curriculum
   by William Toombs and William Tierney

1990 ASHE-ERIC Higher Education Reports

1. The Campus Green: Fund Raising in Higher Education
   Barbara E. Brittingham and Thomas R. Pezzullo

2. The Emeritus Professor: Old Rank - New Meaning
   James E. Mauch, Jack W. Birch, and Jack Matthews

3. "High Risk" Students in Higher Education: Future Trends
   Dionne J. Jones and Betty Collier Watson

4. Budgeting for Higher Education at the State Level: Enigma, Paradox, and Ritual
   Daniel T. Layzell and Jan W. Lyddon

5. Proprietary Schools: Programs, Policies, and Prospects
   John B. Lee and Jamie P. Merisotis

6. College Choice: Understanding Student Enrollment Behavior
   Michael B. Paulsen

7. Pursuing Diversity: Recruiting College Minority Students
   Barbara Astone and Elsa Nuñez-Wormack

8. Social Consciousness and Career Awareness: Emerging Link in Higher Education
   John S. Swift, Jr.

1989 ASHE-ERIC Higher Education Reports

1. Making Sense of Administrative Leadership: The 'L' Word in Higher Education
   Estela M. Bensimon, Anna Neumann, and Robert Birnbaum

2. Affirmative Rhetoric, Negative Action: African-American and Hispanic Faculty at Predominantly White Universities
   Valora Washington and William Harvey

3. Postsecondary Developmental Programs: A Traditional Agenda with New Imperatives
   Louise M. Tomlinson

4. The Old College Try: Balancing Athletics and Academics in Higher Education
   John R. Thelin and Lawrence L. Wiseman

5. The Challenge of Diversity: Involvement or Alienation in the Academy?
   Daryl G. Smith

6. Student Goals for College and Courses: A Missing Link in Assessing and Improving Academic Achievement
   Joan S. Stark, Kathleen M. Shaw, and Malcolm A. Lowther

7. The Student as Commuter: Developing a Comprehensive Institutional Response
   Barbara Jacoby

8. Renewing Civic Capacity: Preparing College Students for Service and Citizenship
   Suzanne W. Morse

1988 ASHE-ERIC Higher Education Reports

1. The Invisible Tapestry: Culture in American Colleges and Universities
   George D. Kuh and Elizabeth J. Whitt

2. Critical Thinking: Theory, Research, Practice, and Possibilities
   Joanne Gainen Kurfiss

3. Developing Academic Programs: The Climate for Innovation
   Daniel T. Seymour

4. Peer Teaching: To Teach is To Learn Twice
   Neal A. Whitman

5. Higher Education and State Governments: Renewed Partnership, Cooperation, or Competition?
   Edward R. Hines

6. Entrepreneurship and Higher Education: Lessons for Colleges, Universities, and Industry
   James S. Fairweather

7. Planning for Microcomputers in Higher Education: Strategies for the Next Generation
   Reynolds Ferrante, John Hayman, Mary Susan Carlson, and Harry Phillips

8. The Challenge for Research in Higher Education: Harmonizing Excellence and Utility
   Alan W. Lindsay and Ruth T. Neumann

1987 ASHE-ERIC Higher Education Reports

1. Incentive Early Retirement Programs for Faculty: Innovative Responses to a Changing Environment
   Jay L. Chronister and Thomas R. Kepple, Jr.

2. Working Effectively with Trustees: Building Cooperative Campus Leadership
   Barbara E. Taylor

3. Formal Recognition of Employer-Sponsored Instruction: Conflict and Collegiality in Postsecondary Education
   Nancy S. Nash and Elizabeth M. Hawthorne

4. Learning Styles: Implications for Improving Educational Practices
   Charles S. Claxton and Patricia H. Murrell

5. Higher Education Leadership: Enhancing Skills through Professional Development Programs
   Sharon A. McDade

6. Higher Education and the Public Trust: Improving Stature in Colleges and Universities
   Richard L. Alfred and Julie Weissman

7. College Student Outcomes Assessment: A Talent Development Perspective
   Maryann Jacobi, Alexander Astin, and Frank Ayala, Jr.

8. Opportunity from Strength: Strategic Planning Clarified with Case Examples
   Robert G. Cope

1986 ASHE-ERIC Higher Education Reports

1. Post-tenure Faculty Evaluation: Threat or Opportunity?
   Christine M. Licata

2. Blue Ribbon Commissions and Higher Education: Changing Academe from the Outside
   Janet R. Johnson and Laurence R. Marcus

3. Responsive Professional Education: Balancing Outcomes and Opportunities
   Joan S. Stark, Malcolm A. Lowther, and Bonnie M.K. Hagerty

4. Increasing Students' Learning: A Faculty Guide to Reducing Stress among Students
   Neal A. Whitman, David C. Spendlove, and Claire H. Clark

5. Student Financial Aid and Women: Equity Dilemma?
   Mary Moran

6. The Master's Degree: Tradition, Diversity, Innovation
   Judith S. Glazer

7. The College, the Constitution, and the Consumer Student: Implications for Policy and Practice
   Robert M. Hendrickson and Annette Gibbs

8. Selecting College and University Personnel: The Quest and the Question
   Richard A. Kaplowitz

1985 ASHE-ERIC Higher Education Reports

1. Flexibility in Academic Staffing: Effective Policies and Practices
   Kenneth P. Mortimer, Marque Bagshaw, and Andrew T. Masland

2. Associations in Action: The Washington, D.C. Higher Education Community
   Harland G. Bloland

3. And on the Seventh Day: Faculty Consulting and Supplemental Income
   Carol M. Boyer and Darrell R. Lewis

4. Faculty Research Performance: Lessons from the Sciences and Social Sciences
   John W. Creswell

5. Academic Program Review: Institutional Approaches, Expectations, and Controversies
   Clifton F. Conrad and Richard F. Wilson

6. Students in Urban Settings: Achieving the Baccalaureate Degree
   Richard C. Richardson, Jr. and Louis W. Bender

7. Serving More Than Students: A Critical Need for College Student Personnel Services
   Peter H. Garland

8. Faculty Participation in Decision Making: Necessity or Luxury?
   Carol E. Floyd

1984 ASHE-ERIC Higher Education Reports

1. Adult Learning: State Policies and Institutional Practices
   K. Patricia Cross and Anne-Marie McCartan

2. Student Stress: Effects and Solutions
   Neal A. Whitman, David C. Spendlove, and Claire H. Clark

3. Part-time Faulty: Higher Education at a Crossroads
   Judith M. Gappa

4. Sex Discrimination Law in Higher Education: The Lessons of the Past Decade. ED 252 169.*
   J. Ralph Lindgren, Patti T. Ota, Perry A. Zirkel, and Nan Van Gieson

5. Faculty Freedoms and Institutional Accountability: Interactions and Conflicts
   Steven G. Olswang and Barbara A. Lee

6. The High Technology Connection: Academic/Industrial Cooperation for Economic Growth
   Lynn G. Johnson

7. Employee Educational Programs: Implications for Industry and Higher Education. ED 258 501.*
   Suzanne W. Morse

8. Academic Libraries: The Changing Knowledge Centers of Colleges and Universities
   Barbara B. Moran

9. Futures Research and the Strategic Planning Process: Implications for Higher Education
   James L. Morrison, William L. Renfro, and Wayne I. Boucher

10. Faculty Workload: Research, Theory, and Interpretation
    Harold E. Yuker

*Out-of-print. Available through EDRS. Call 1-800-443-ERIC.

Quantity **Amount**

_____ Please begin my subscription to the 1991 *ASHE-ERIC Higher Education Reports* at $90.00, 33% off the cover price, starting with Report 1, 1991.

_____

_____ Please send a complete set of the 1990 *ASHE-ERIC Higher Education Reports* at $80.00, 41% off the cover price.

_____

_____ Outside the U.S., add $10.00 per series for postage.

_____

Individual reports are avilable at the following prices:

1990 and 1991, $17.00	1983 and 1984, $7.50
1988 and 1989, $15.00	1982 and back, $6.50
1985 to 1987, $10.00	

Book rate postage within the U.S. is included. Outside U.S., please add $1.00 per book for postage. Fast U.P.S. shipping is available within the contiguous U.S. at $2.50 for each order under $50.00, and calculated at 5% of invoice total for orders $50.00 or above. All orders under $45.00 must be prepaid.

PLEASE SEND ME THE FOLLOWING REPORTS:

Quantity	Report No.	Year	Title	Amount

Subtotal:	
Foreign or UPS:	
Total Due:	

Please check one of the following:
- ☐ Check enclosed, payable to GWU–ERIC.
- ☐ Purchase order attached ($45.00 minimum).
- ☐ Charge my credit card indicated below:
  - ☐ Visa   ☐ MasterCard

Expiration Date _____

Name _____

Title _____

Institution _____

Address _____

City _____ State _____ Zip _____

Phone _____

Signature _____ Date _____

SEND ALL ORDERS TO:
ASHE-ERIC Higher Education Reports
The George Washington University
One Dupont Circle, Suite 630
Washington, DC 20036-1183
Phone: (202) 296-2597